Christ's Words

Taken from the Good News Bible
with a foreword by
The Very Reverend Professor Thomas F. Torrance

Published by   Bible Society
on behalf of The Order of Christian Unity
© BFBS 1980

Text from the Good News Bible
Published by the Bible Societies and William Collins
© American Bible Society, New York 1966, 1971, 1976
BFBS 1980 10M   TEV673/115   ISBN 0 564 04162 9

Printed in Great Britain by Biddles Ltd, Guildford, Surrey

Introduction

'Christ's Words' contains all the words of Jesus as recorded in the New Testament. It will help you see quickly what He said about all manner of things, from who He was to problems which affect our everyday life.

You will notice that each page is divided into two columns. On the left, you will find a heading and a group of references. These will tell you exactly where in the New Testament you can read the story or happening about which Jesus is speaking. In the right hand section you will see a short sentence in italics which sets the scene for you, and then come the words of Jesus as they appear in the Good News Bible.

This book has been published by the Bible Society on behalf of the Order of Christian Unity. The names of the Editorial Board involved in its preparation are found opposite.

Foreword

The Very Rev. Thomas F. Torrance
Professor of Christian Dogmatics, University of Edinburgh

Throughout the centuries Christians have leapt to their feet as
the Holy Gospel is read at the celebration of the Eucharist,
in joyful, spontaneous reverence of the Word of Christ Himself,
as it has been handed down to us from Apostolic times in the
four books of the New Testament we know as *Matthew, Mark,
Luke* and *John*. It was this direct impact of the teaching of our
Lord that was so creative and formative of the Christian life
from the very beginning of the Church.

In modern times this impact has been somewhat blunted
through a changed attitude to the sheer majesty of the Gospels
that has resulted from historio-critical research. The intention
of this research has been to confront us today across the
centuries with the original Jesus, undiluted and unobstructed by
layers of interpretative material with which His teaching has
so often been overlaid. Yet it is now more and more evident
that the claims we have made for 'assured results' from our
critical research are greatly exaggerated. In our interpretative
criticism we have been insufficiently aware of the fact that the
results of our research have been determined from behind by
hidden assumptions and presuppositions derived from a modern
and very different culture which we have been reading into the
New Testament, so that too often we ourselves are guilty of
overlaying the original Jesus with distorting interpretations of
our own. Now that these hidden assumptions are being brought
to view and are found again and again to be untenable in the
light of rigorous scientific analysis, many of us are increasingly
convinced that the traditional form of the Gospels commands our
acknowledgment, making us want to listen to the Words of Jesus
in the coherent patterns in which they were set in the formation
of the evangelical tradition. It was after all in this traditional
form that the Gospels were so marvellously effective in the
establishment and shaping of the Christian Church as it took
root in our human culture in the early centuries of our era. It
was then and in that way that the Gospel conquered the world

and the name of Christ was sealed upon generation after generation.

There is thus every reason for us to welcome a presentation of the teaching of Christ as it is given in the Gospels, in its undiluted and uncompromising form, which is accessible to the general reader. There is admittedly some loss in the way in which the Words of Christ are here detached from His miraculous acts in life and passion and resurrection, and thus are taken out of the narrative setting provided by the four Gospels where we find the same teaching given with appropriate variations in different contexts and life-situations. But there is also great gain in the way in which this little work brings together the teaching of Jesus as it has been handed down to us, for it is thus thrown into sharp relief in its simplicity and directness. Here a fresh, challenging confrontation between the Word of Christ and the modern reader is effected. This comes over very powerfully in the version of the *Good News Bible* which I myself find the most helpful of the modern renderings for both private and public lection.

May our Lord Himself accompany the reading of His Words thus presented with the blessing of His own Spirit, so that our own generation may in this way hear Christ speaking with new directness and force.

Thomas F. Torrance

Christ's Words

in Matthew

Christ's Words in Matthew

The Baptism of Jesus
Mt 3.15

When John questioned his right to baptize Him
Let it be so for now. For in this way we shall do all that God requires.

The Temptation of Jesus
Mt 4.4,7,10

As He was being tempted by the Devil, to turn stones into bread
The scripture says, 'Man cannot live on bread alone, but needs every word that God speaks.'

To throw Himself down from the Temple
But the scripture also says, 'Do not put the Lord your God to the test.'

And to kneel down and worship Satan
Go away, Satan! The scripture says, 'Worship the Lord your God and serve only him!'

Jesus Begins His Work in Galilee
Mt 4.17

As he began to give His message in Galilee
Turn away from your sins, because the Kingdom of heaven is near!

Jesus Calls Four Fishermen
Mt 4.19

When He called Simon and Andrew
Come with me, and I will teach you to catch men.

THE SERMON ON THE MOUNT

True Happiness
Mt 5.3–12

To the crowds and disciples as He preached to them on the hillside
Happy are those who know they are spiritually poor;
  the Kingdom of heaven belongs to them.
Happy are those who mourn;
  God will comfort them!
Happy are those who are humble;
  they will receive what God has promised!
Happy are those whose greatest desire is to do what God requires;
  God will satisfy them fully!
Happy are those who are merciful to others;
  God will be merciful to them!
Happy are the pure in heart;
  they will see God!
Happy are those who work for peace;

God will call them his children!
Happy are those who are persecuted because they do what God
    requires;
the Kingdom of heaven belongs to them!

Happy are you when people insult you and persecute you and
tell all kinds of evil lies against you because you are my
followers. Be happy and glad, for a great reward is kept for you
in heaven. This is how the prophets who lived before you were
persecuted.

Salt and Light
Mt 5.13–16

You are like salt for all mankind. But if salt loses its saltiness,
there is no way to make it salty again. It has become worthless,
so it is thrown out and people trample on it.

You are like light for the whole world. A city built on a hill
cannot be hidden. No one lights a lamp and puts it under a
bowl; instead he puts it on the lampstand, where it gives light
for everyone in the house. In the same way your light must shine
before people, so that they will see the good things you do and
praise your Father in heaven.

Teaching about the Law
Mt 5.17–20

Do not think that I have come to do away with the Law of
Moses and the teachings of the prophets. I have not come to do
away with them, but to make their teachings come true.
Remember that as long as heaven and earth last, not the least
point nor the smallest detail of the Law will be done away with
– not until the end of all things. So then, whoever disobeys even
the least important of the commandments and teaches others to
do the same, will be least in the Kingdom of heaven. On the
other hand, whoever obeys the Law and teaches others to do the
same, will be great in the Kingdom of heaven. I tell you, then,
that you will be able to enter the Kingdom of heaven only if you
are more faithful than the teachers of the Law and the Pharisees
in doing what God requires.

Teaching about Anger
Mt 5.21–26

You have heard that people were told in the past, 'Do not
commit murder; anyone who does will be brought to trial.' But
now I tell you: whoever is angry with his brother will be brought
to trial, whoever calls his brother 'You good-for-nothing!' will be
brought before the Council, and whoever calls his brother a
worthless fool will be in danger of going to the fire of hell. So if
you are about to offer your gift to God at the altar and there you

remember that your brother has something against you, leave your gift there in front of the altar, go at once and make peace with your brother, and then come back and offer your gift to God.

If someone brings a lawsuit against you and takes you to court, settle the dispute with him while there is time, before you get to court. Once you are there, he will hand you over to the judge, who will hand you over to the police, and you will be put in jail. There you will stay, I tell you, until you pay the last penny of your fine.

Teaching about Adultery
Mt 5.27–30

You have heard that it was said, 'Do not commit adultery.' But now I tell you: anyone who looks at a woman and wants to possess her is guilty of committing adultery with her in his heart. So if your right eye causes you to sin, take it out and throw it away! It is much better for you to lose a part of your body than to have your whole body thrown into hell. If your right hand causes you to sin, cut it off and throw it away! It is much better for you to lose one of your limbs than for your whole body to go to hell.

Teaching about Divorce
Mt 5.31–32

It was also said, 'Anyone who divorces his wife must give her a written notice of divorce.' But now I tell you: if a man divorces his wife, even though she has not been unfaithful, then he is guilty of making her commit adultery if she marries again; and the man who marries her commits adultery also.

Teaching about Vows
Mt 5.33–37

You have also heard that people were told in the past, 'Do not break your promise, but do what you have vowed to the Lord to do.' But now I tell you: do not use any vow when you make a promise. Do not swear by heaven, because it is God's throne; nor by earth, because it is the resting place for his feet; nor by Jerusalem, because it is the city of the great King. Do not even swear by your head, because you cannot make a single hair white or black. Just say 'Yes' or 'No' – anything else you say comes from the Evil One.

Teaching about Revenge
Mt 5.38–42

You have heard that it was said, 'An eye for an eye, and a tooth for a tooth.' But now I tell you: do not take revenge on someone who wrongs you. If anyone slaps you on the right cheek, let him slap your left cheek too. And if someone takes you to court to sue you for your shirt, let him have your coat as well. And if one of the occupation troops forces you to carry his pack one kilometre, carry it two kilometres. When someone asks you for something, give it to him; when someone wants to borrow something, lend it to him.

Love for Enemies
Mt 5.43–48

You have heard that it was said, 'Love your friends, hate your enemies.' But now I tell you: love your enemies and pray for those who persecute you, so that you may become the sons of your Father in heaven. For he makes his sun to shine on bad and good people alike, and gives rain to those who do good and to those who do evil. Why should God reward you if you love only the people who love you? Even the tax collectors do that! And if you speak only to your friends, have you done anything out of the ordinary? Even the pagans do that! You must be perfect – just as your Father in heaven is perfect!

Teaching about Charity
Mt 6.1–4

Make certain you do not perform your religious duties in public so that people will see what you do. If you do these things publicly, you will not have any reward from your Father in heaven.

So when you give something to a needy person, do not make a big show of it, as the hypocrites do in the houses of worship and on the streets. They do it so that people will praise them. I assure you, they have already been paid in full. But when you help a needy person, do it in such a way that even your closest friend will not know about it. Then it will be a private matter. And your Father, who sees what you do in private, will reward you.

Teaching about Prayer
Mt 6.5–15

When you pray, do not be like the hypocrites! They love to stand up and pray in the houses of worship and on the street corners, so that everyone will see them. I assure you, they have already been paid in full. But when you pray, go to your room, close the door, and pray to your Father, who is unseen. And your Father, who sees what you do in private, will reward you.

When you pray, do not use a lot of meaningless words, as the pagans do, who think that God will hear them because their prayers are long. Do not be like them. Your Father already knows what you need before you ask him. This, then, is how you should pray:

'Our Father in heaven:
    May your holy name be honoured;
    may your Kingdom come;
    may your will be done on earth as it is in heaven.
    Give us today the food we need.
    Forgive us the wrongs we have done,
        as we forgive the wrongs that others have done to us.
    Do not bring us to hard testing,
        but keep us safe from the Evil One.'

If you forgive others the wrongs they have done to you, your Father in heaven will also forgive you. But if you do not forgive others, then your Father will not forgive the wrongs you have done.

Teaching about Fasting
Mt 6.16–18

And when you fast, do not put on a sad face as the hypocrites do. They neglect their appearance so that everyone will see that they are fasting. I assure you, they have already been paid in full. When you go without food, wash your face and comb your hair, so that others cannot know that you are fasting – only your Father, who is unseen, will know. And your Father, who sees what you do in private, will reward you.

Riches in Heaven
Mt 6.19–21

Do not store up riches for yourselves here on earth, where moths and rust destroy, and robbers break in and steal. Instead, store up riches for yourselves in heaven, where moths and rust cannot destroy, and robbers cannot break in and steal. For your heart will always be where your riches are.

The Light of the Body
Mt 6.22–23

The eyes are like a lamp for the body. If your eyes are sound, your whole body will be full of light; but if your eyes are no good, your body will be in darkness. So if the light in you is darkness, how terribly dark it will be!

God and Possessions
Mt 6.24–34

No one can be a slave of two masters; he will hate one and love the other; he will be loyal to one and despise the other. You cannot serve both God and money.

This is why I tell you not to be worried about the food and drink you need in order to stay alive, or about clothes for your body. After all, isn't life worth more than food? And isn't the body worth more than clothes? Look at the birds flying around: they do not sow seeds, gather a harvest and put it in barns; yet your Father in heaven takes care of them! Aren't you worth much more than birds? Can any of you live a bit longer by worrying about it?

And why worry about clothes? Look how the wild flowers grow: they do not work or make clothes for themselves. But I tell you that not even King Solomon with all his wealth had clothes as beautiful as one of these flowers. It is God who clothes the wild grass – grass that is here today and gone tomorrow, burnt up in the oven. Won't he be all the more sure to clothe you? How little faith you have!

So do not start worrying: 'Where will my food come from? or my drink? or my clothes?' (These are the things the pagans are always concerned about.) Your Father in heaven knows that you need all these things. Instead, be concerned above everything else with the Kingdom of God and with what he requires of you, and he will provide you with all these other things. So do not worry about tomorrow; it will have enough worries of its own. There is no need to add to the troubles each day brings.

Judging Others
Mt 7.1–6

Do not judge others, so that God will not judge you, for God will judge you in the same way as you judge others, and he will apply to you the same rules you apply to others. Why, then, do you look at the speck in your brother's eye, and pay no attention to the log in your own eye? How dare you say to your brother, 'Please, let me take that speck out of your eye,' when you have a log in your own eye? You hypocrite! First take the log out of your own eye, and then you will be able to see clearly to take the speck out of your brother's eye.

Do not give what is holy to dogs – they will only turn and attack you. Do not throw your pearls in front of pigs – they will only trample them underfoot.

Ask, Seek, Knock
Mt 7.7–12

Ask, and you will receive; seek, and you will find; knock, and the door will be opened to you. For everyone who asks will receive, and anyone who seeks will find, and the door will be opened to him who knocks. Would any of you who are fathers give your son a stone when he asks for bread? Or would you give him a snake when he asks for a fish? Bad as you are, you know how to give good things to your children. How much more, then, will your Father in heaven give good things to those who ask him!

Do for others what you want them to do for you: this is the meaning of the Law of Moses and of the teachings of the prophets.

The Narrow Gate
Mt 7.13–14

Go in through the narrow gate, because the gate to hell is wide and the road that leads to it is easy, and there are many who travel it. But the gate to life is narrow and the way that leads to it is hard, and there are few people who find it.

A Tree and its Fruit
Mt 7.15–20

Be on your guard against false prophets; they come to you looking like sheep on the outside, but on the inside they are really like wild wolves. You will know them by what they do. Thorn bushes do not bear grapes, and briars do not bear figs. A healthy tree bears good fruit, but a poor tree bears bad fruit. A healthy tree cannot bear bad fruit, and a poor tree cannot bear good fruit. And any tree that does not bear good fruit is cut down and thrown in the fire. So then, you will know the false prophets by what they do.

I Never Knew You
Mt 7.21–23

Not everyone who calls me 'Lord, Lord' will enter the Kingdom of heaven, but only those who do what my Father in heaven wants them to do. When Judgement Day comes, many will say to me, 'Lord, Lord! In your name we spoke God's message, by your name we drove out many demons and performed many miracles!' Then I will say to them, 'I never knew you. Get away from me, you wicked people!'

The Two House Builders
Mt 7.24–27

So then, anyone who hears these words of mine and obeys them is like a wise man who built his house on rock. The rain poured down, the rivers overflowed, and the wind blew hard against that house. But it did not fall, because it was built on rock.

But anyone who hears these words of mine and does not obey them is like a foolish man who built his house on sand. The rain poured down, the rivers overflowed, the wind blew hard against that house, and it fell. And what a terrible fall that was!

Jesus Heals a Man
Mt 8.3,4

When a man with a dreaded skin-disease told Him He could make him clean if He wanted to
I do want to. Be clean!

And when the man was healed at once
Listen! Don't tell anyone, but go straight to the priest and let

him examine you; then in order to prove to everyone that you are cured, offer the sacrifice that Moses ordered.

Jesus Heals a Roman Officer's Servant
Mt 8.7,10–12,13

To a Roman officer who asked Him to heal his servant
I will go and make him well.

To the people concerning the officer's faith
I tell you, I have never found anyone in Israel with faith like this. I assure you that many will come from the east and the west and sit down with Abraham, Isaac, and Jacob at the feast in the Kingdom of heaven. But those who should be in the Kingdom will be thrown out into the darkness where they will cry and grind their teeth.

To the officer
Go home, and what you believe will be done for you.

The Would-be Followers of Jesus
Mt 8.20,22

To a teacher of the Law who wanted to follow Him
Foxes have holes, and birds have nests, but the Son of Man has nowhere to lie down and rest.

And to a disciple who wanted first to bury his father
Follow me, and let the dead bury their own dead.

Jesus Calms a Storm
Mt 8.26

To His disciples who were afraid, in a boat during a storm
Why are you so frightened? How little faith you have!

Jesus Heals Two Men with Demons
Mt 8.32

To demons who begged Him to send them into a herd of pigs if they were to be driven out of two men
Go.

Jesus Heals a Paralysed Man
Mt 9.2,4–6

When a paralysed man was brought to Him
Courage, my son! Your sins are forgiven.

To some teachers of the Law who then accused Him of blasphemy
Why are you thinking such evil things? Is it easier to say, 'Your sins are forgiven,' or to say, 'Get up and walk'? I will prove to you, then, that the Son of Man has authority on earth to forgive sins.

And to the man again
Get up, pick up your bed, and go home!

Jesus Calls Matthew
Mt 9.9

As He called Matthew, a tax collector
Follow me.

Mt 9.12,13

To some Pharisees who asked why He ate with tax collectors and other outcasts
People who are well do not need a doctor, but only those who are sick. Go and find out what is meant by the scripture that says: 'It is kindness that I want, not animal sacrifices.' I have not come to call respectable people, but outcasts.

The Question about Fasting
Mt 9.15–17

To the followers of John the Baptist when they asked why His disciples did not fast
Do you expect the guests at a wedding party to be sad as long as the bridegroom is with them? Of course not! But the day will come when the bridegroom will be taken away from them, and then they will fast.

No one patches up an old coat with a piece of new cloth, for the new patch will shrink and make an even bigger hole in the coat. Nor does anyone pour new wine into used wineskins, for the skins will burst, the wine will pour out, and the skins will be ruined. Instead new wine is poured into fresh wineskins, and both will keep in good condition.

The Official's Daughter and the Woman Who Touched Jesus' Cloak
Mt 9.22,24

To the woman who had suffered from severe bleeding for 12 years and who touched the edge of His cloak, believing she would be healed
Courage, my daughter! Your faith has made you well.

To the people gathered to mourn the death of a Jewish official's young daughter
Get out, everybody! The little girl is not dead – she is only sleeping.

Jesus Heals Two Blind Men
Mt 9.28,29,30

To two blind men who came to Him to be healed
Do you believe that I can heal you?

When they said they did
Let it happen then, just as you believe!

And after they had been healed
Don't tell this to anyone.

Jesus Has Pity for the People
Mt 9.37,38

To His disciples, after He had gone round the towns and villages, teaching and healing, and was filled with pity for the crowds He saw
The harvest is large, but there are few workers to gather it in. Pray to the owner of the harvest that he will send out workers to gather in his harvest.

The Mission of the Twelve
Mt 10.5–15

As He instructed His twelve disciples before sending them out on their own
Do not go to any Gentile territory or any Samaritan towns. Instead, you are to go to those lost sheep, the people of Israel. Go and preach, 'The Kingdom of heaven is near!' Heal the sick, bring the dead back to life, heal those who suffer from dreaded skin-diseases, and drive out demons. You have received without paying, so give without being paid. Do not carry any gold, silver, or copper money in your pockets; do not carry a beggar's bag for the journey or an extra shirt or shoes or a stick. A worker should be given what he needs.

When you come to a town or village, go in and look for someone who is willing to welcome you, and stay with him until you leave that place. When you go into a house, say 'Peace be with you.' If the people in that house welcome you, let your greeting of peace remain; but if they do not welcome you, then take back your greeting. And if some home or town will not welcome you or listen to you, then leave that place and shake the dust off your feet. I assure you that on the Judgement Day God will show more mercy to the people of Sodom and Gomorrah than to the people of that town!

Coming Persecutions
Mt 10.16–25

Listen! I am sending you out just like sheep to a pack of wolves. You must be as cautious as snakes and as gentle as doves. Watch out, for there will be men who will arrest you and take you to court, and they will whip you in the synagogues. For my sake you will be brought to trial before rulers and kings, to tell the Good News to them and to the Gentiles. When they bring you to trial, do not worry about what you are going to say or how you will say it; when the time comes, you will be given what you will say. For the words you will speak will not be yours; they will come from the Spirit of your Father speaking through you.

Men will hand over their own brothers to be put to death, and fathers will do the same to their children; children will turn against their parents and have them put to death. Everyone will hate you because of me. But whoever holds out to the end will be saved. When they persecute you in one town, run away to another one. I assure you that you will not finish your work in all the towns of Israel before the Son of Man comes.

No pupil is greater than his teacher; no slave is greater than his master. So a pupil should be satisfied to become like his teacher, and a slave like his master. If the head of the family is called Beelzebul, the members of the family will be called even worse names!

Whom to Fear
Mt 10.26–31

So do not be afraid of people. Whatever is now covered up will be uncovered and every secret will be made known. What I am telling you in the dark you must repeat in broad daylight, and what you have heard in private you must announce from the housetops. Do not be afraid of those who kill the body but cannot kill the soul; rather be afraid of God, who can destroy both body and soul in hell. For only a penny you can buy two sparrows, yet not one sparrow falls to the ground without your Father's consent. As for you, even the hairs of your head have all been counted. So do not be afraid; you are worth much more than many sparrows!

Confessing and Rejecting Christ
Mt 10.32–33

If anyone declares publicly that he belongs to me, I will do the same for him before my Father in heaven. But if anyone rejects me publicly, I will reject him before my Father in heaven.

Not Peace, but a Sword
Mt 10.34–39

Do not think that I have come to bring peace to the world. No, I did not come to bring peace, but a sword. I came to set sons against their fathers, daughters against their mothers, daughters-in-law against their mothers-in-law; a man's worst enemies will be the members of his own family.

Whoever loves his father or mother more than me is not fit to be my disciple; whoever loves his son or daughter more than me is not fit to be my disciple. Whoever does not take up his cross and follow in my steps is not fit to be my disciple. Whoever tries to gain his own life will lose it; but whoever loses his life for my sake will gain it.

Rewards
Mt 10.40–42

Whoever welcomes you welcomes me; and whoever welcomes me welcomes the one who sent me. Whoever welcomes God's messenger because he is God's messenger, will share in his reward. And whoever welcomes a good man because he is good, will share in his reward. You can be sure that whoever gives even a drink of cold water to one of the least of these my followers because he is my follower, will certainly receive a reward.

The Messengers from John the Baptist
Mt 11.4–6,7–19

To John's disciples when they asked Him if He was the one John said was going to come, or if they were to expect someone else.
Go back and tell John what you are hearing and seeing: the blind can see, the lame can walk, those who suffer from dreaded skin-diseases are made clean, the deaf hear, the dead are brought back to life, and the Good News is preached to the poor. How happy are those who have no doubts about me!

To the crowds
When you went out to John in the desert, what did you expect to see? A blade of grass bending in the wind? What did you go out to see? A man dressed up in fancy clothes? People who dress like that live in palaces! Tell me, what did you go out to see? A prophet? Yes indeed, but you saw much more than a prophet. For John is the one of whom the scripture says: 'God said, I will send my messenger ahead of you to open the way for you.' I assure you that John the Baptist is greater than any man who has ever lived. But he who is least in the Kingdom of heaven is greater than John. From the time John preached his message until this very day the Kingdom of heaven has suffered violent attacks, and violent men try to seize it. Until the time of John all the prophets and the Law of Moses spoke about the Kingdom; and if you are willing to believe their message, John is Elijah, whose coming was predicted. Listen, then, if you have ears!

Now, to what can I compare the people of this day? They are like children sitting in the market-place. One group shouts to the other, 'We played wedding music for you, but you wouldn't dance! We sang funeral songs, but you wouldn't cry!' When John came, he fasted and drank no wine, and everyone said, 'He has a demon in him!' When the Son of Man came, he ate and drank, and everyone said, 'Look at this man! He is a glutton and a drinker, a friend of tax collectors and other outcasts!' God's wisdom, however, is shown to be true by its results.

The Unbelieving Towns
Mt 11.21–24

To the people of Chorazin and Bethsaida who did not believe in Him
How terrible it will be for you, Chorazin! How terrible for

you too, Bethsaida! If the miracles which were performed in you had been performed in Tyre and Sidon, the people there would long ago have put on sackcloth and sprinkled ashes on themselves, to show that they had turned from their sins! I assure you that on the Judgement Day God will show more mercy to the people of Tyre and Sidon than to you! And as for you, Capernaum! Did you want to lift yourself up to heaven? You will be thrown down to hell! If the miracles which were performed in you had been performed in Sodom, it would still be in existence today! You can be sure that on the Judgement Day God will show more mercy to Sodom than to you!

Come to Me and Rest
Mt 11.25–26,27–30

To His Father
Father, Lord of heaven and earth! I thank you because you have shown to the unlearned what you have hidden from the wise and learned. Yes, Father, this was how you wanted it to happen.

And to the people
My Father has given me all things. No one knows the Son except the Father, and no one knows the Father except the Son and those to whom the Son chooses to reveal him.

Come to me, all of you who are tired from carrying heavy loads, and I will give you rest. Take my yoke and put it on you, and learn from me, because I am gentle and humble in spirit; and you will find rest. For the yoke I will give you is easy, and the load I will put on you is light.

The Question about the Sabbath
Mt 12.3–8

To the Pharisees who complained that His disciples had picked ears of corn and eaten the grain on the Sabbath
Have you never read what David did that time when he and his men were hungry? He went into the house of God, and he and his men ate the bread offered to God, even though it was against the Law for them to eat it – only the priests were allowed to eat that bread. Or have you not read in the Law of Moses that every Sabbath the priests in the Temple actually break the Sabbath law, yet they are not guilty? I tell you that there is something here greater than the Temple. The scripture says, 'It is kindness that I want, not animal sacrifices.' If you really knew what this means, you would not condemn people who are not guilty; for the Son of Man is Lord of the Sabbath.

**The Man
with a Paralysed Hand**
Mt 12.11–13

To the Pharisees who objected to His healing people on the Sabbath
What if one of you has a sheep and it falls into a deep hole on
the Sabbath? Will he not take hold of it and lift it out? And a
man is worth much more than a sheep! So then, our Law does
allow us to help someone on the Sabbath.

And to the man who prompted the discussion
Stretch out your hand.

Jesus and Beelzebul
Mt 12.25–32

*To the Pharisees who said He drove out demons through the power of
Beelzebul*
Any country that divides itself into groups which fight each other
will not last very long. And any town or family that divides itself
into groups which fight each other will fall apart. So if one group
is fighting another in Satan's kingdom, this means that it is
already divided into groups and will soon fall apart! You say
that I drive out demons because Beelzebul gives me the power to
do so. Well, then, who gives your followers the power to drive
them out? What your own followers do proves that you are
wrong! No, it is not Beelzebul, but God's Spirit, who gives me
the power to drive out demons, which proves that the Kingdom
of God has already come upon you.

No one can break into a strong man's house and take away his
belongings unless he first ties up the strong man; then he can
plunder his house.

Anyone who is not for me is really against me; anyone who does
not help me gather is really scattering. And so I tell you that
people can be forgiven any sin and any evil thing they say; but
whoever says evil things against the Holy Spirit will not be
forgiven. Anyone who says something against the Son of Man
can be forgiven; but whoever says something against the Holy
Spirit will not be forgiven – now or ever.

A Tree and Its Fruit
Mt 12.33–37

To have good fruit you must have a healthy tree; if you have a
poor tree, you will have bad fruit. A tree is known by the kind of
fruit it bears. You snakes – how can you say good things when
you are evil? For the mouth speaks what the heart is full of. A
good person brings good things out of his treasure of good
things; a bad person brings bad things out of his treasure of bad
things.

You can be sure that on Judgement Day everyone will have to give account of every useless word he has every spoken. Your words will be used to judge you – to declare you either innocent or guilty.

The Demand for a Miracle
Mt 12.39–42

To some teachers of the Law and some Pharisees when they asked for a miracle
How evil and godless are the people of this day! You ask me for a miracle? No! The only miracle you will be given is the miracle of the prophet Jonah. In the same way that Jonah spent three days and nights in the big fish, so will the Son of Man spend three days and nights in the depths of the earth. On Judgement Day the people of Nineveh will stand up and accuse you, because they turned from their sins when they heard Jonah preach; and I tell you that there is something here greater than Jonah! On Judgement Day the Queen of Sheba will stand up and accuse you, because she travelled all the way from her country to listen to King Solomon's wise teaching; and I assure you that there is something here greater than Solomon!

The Return of the Evil Spirit
Mt 12.43–45

Concerning the fate of evil people
When an evil spirit goes out of a person, it travels over dry country looking for a place to rest. If it can't find one, it says to itself, 'I will go back to my house.' So it goes back and finds the house empty, clean, and all tidy. Then it goes out and brings along seven other spirits even worse than itself, and they come and live there. So when it is all over, that person is in a worse state than he was at the beginning. This is what will happen to the evil people of this day.

Jesus' Mother and Brothers
Mt 12.47–50

When He was told that His mother and brothers were standing outside wanting to speak to Him
Who is my mother? Who are my brothers? Look! Here are my mother and my brothers! Whoever does what my Father in heaven wants him to do is my brother, my sister, and my mother.

The Parable of the Sower
Mt 13.3–9

To the people as He told them parables by the lake-side
Once there was a man who went out to sow corn. As he scattered the seed in the field, some of it fell along the path, and the birds came and ate it up. Some of it fell on rocky ground, where there was little soil. The seeds soon sprouted, because the soil wasn't deep. But when the sun came up, it burnt the young

plants; and because the roots had not grown deep enough, the plants soon dried up. Some of the seed fell among thorn bushes, which grew up and choked the plants. But some seeds fell in good soil, and the plants produced corn; some produced a hundred grains, others sixty and others thirty. Listen, then, if you have ears!

The Purpose of the Parables
Mt 13.11–17

To His disciples who asked Him why He taught in parables
The knowledge about the secrets of the Kingdom of heaven has been given to you, but not to them. For the person who has something will be given more, so that he will have more than enough; but the person who has nothing will have taken away from him even the little he has. The reason I use parables in talking to them is that they look, but do not see, and they listen, but do not hear or understand. So the prophecy of Isaiah applies to them:

'This people will listen and listen, but not understand;
   they will look and look, but not see,
because their minds are dull,
   and they have stopped up their ears
   and have closed their eyes.
Otherwise, their eyes would see,
   their ears would hear,
   their minds would understand,
   and they would turn to me, says God,
   and I would heal them.'

As for you, how fortunate you are! Your eyes see and your ears hear. I assure you that many prophets and many of God's people wanted very much to see what you see, but they could not, and to hear what you hear, but they did not.

**Jesus Explains
the Parable of the Sower**
Mt 13.18–23

Listen, then, and learn what the parable of the sower means. Those who hear the message about the Kingdom but do not understand it are like the seeds that fell along the path. The Evil One comes and snatches away what was sown in them. The seeds that fell on rocky ground stand for those who receive the message gladly as soon as they hear it. But it does not sink deep into them, and they don't last long. So when trouble or persecution comes because of the message, they give up at once. The seeds that fell among thorn bushes stand for those who hear the message; but the worries about this life and the love for riches choke the message, and they don't bear fruit. And the seeds sown in the good soil stand for those who hear the message and understand it; they bear fruit, some as much as a hundred, others sixty, and others thirty.

The Parable of the Weeds
Mt 13.24–30

As He continued to teach in parables
The Kingdom of heaven is like this. A man sowed good seed in his field. One night, when everyone was asleep, an enemy came and sowed weeds among the wheat and went away. When the plants grew and the ears of corn began to form, then the weeds showed up. The man's servants came to him and said, 'Sir, it was good seed you sowed in your field; where did the weeds come from?' 'It was some enemy who did this,' he answered. 'Do you want us to go and pull up the weeds?' they asked him. 'No,' he answered, 'because as you gather the weeds you might pull up some of the wheat along with them. Let the wheat and the weeds both grow together until harvest. Then I will tell the harvest workers to pull up the weeds first, tie them in bundles and burn them and then to gather in the wheat and put it in my barn.'

The Parable of the Mustard Seed
Mt 13.31–32

The Kingdom of heaven is like this. A man takes a mustard seed and sows it in his field. It is the smallest of all seeds, but when it grows up, it is the biggest of all plants. It becomes a tree, so that birds come and make their nests in its branches.

The Parable of the Yeast
Mt 13.33

The Kingdom of heaven is like this. A woman takes some yeast and mixes it with forty litres of flour until the whole batch of dough rises.

Jesus Explains the Parable of the Weeds
Mt 13.37–43

To His disciples who asked Him the meaning of the parable of the weeds
The man who sowed the good seed is the Son of Man; the field is the world; the good seed is the people who belong to the Kingdom; the weeds are the people who belong to the Evil One; and the enemy who sowed the weeds is the Devil. The harvest is the end of the age, and the harvest workers are angels. Just as the weeds are gathered up and burnt in the fire, so the same thing will happen at the end of the age: the Son of Man will send out his angels to gather up out of his Kingdom all those who cause people to sin and all others who do evil things, and they will throw them into the fiery furnace, where they will cry and grind their teeth. Then God's people will shine like the sun in their Father's Kingdom. Listen, then, if you have ears!

| The Parable of the Hidden Treasure Mt 13.44 | The Kingdom of heaven is like this. A man happens to find a treasure hidden in a field. He covers it up again, and is so happy that he goes and sells everything he has, and then goes back and buys that field. |

The Parable of the Hidden Treasure
Mt 13.44

The Kingdom of heaven is like this. A man happens to find a treasure hidden in a field. He covers it up again, and is so happy that he goes and sells everything he has, and then goes back and buys that field.

The Parable of the Pearl
Mt 13.45–46

Also, the Kingdom of heaven is like this. A man is looking for fine pearls, and when he finds one that is unusually fine, he goes and sells everything he has, and buys that pearl.

The Parable of the Net
Mt 13.47–50

Also, the Kingdom of heaven is like this. Some fishermen throw their net out in the lake and catch all kinds of fish. When the net is full, they pull it to shore and sit down to divide the fish; the good ones go into their buckets, the worthless ones are thrown away. It will be like this at the end of the age: the angels will go out and gather up the evil people from among the good and will throw them into the fiery furnace, where they will cry and grind their teeth.

New Truths and Old
Mt 13.51,52

After His series of parables about the Kingdom of heaven
Do you understand these things?

When they said they did
This means, then, that every teacher of the Law who becomes a disciple in the Kingdom of heaven is like the owner of a house who takes new and old things out of his storeroom.

Jesus is Rejected at Nazareth
Mt 13.57

In the synagogue at Nazareth, His home town, where He was rejected by the people
A prophet is respected everywhere except in his home town and by his own family.

Jesus Feeds Five Thousand Men
Mt 14.16,18

When His disciples showed concern for a large, hungry crowd which had followed Him all day as He taught and healed
They don't have to leave. You yourselves give them something to eat!

And when they said they had only five loaves and two fish
Then bring them here to me.

Jesus Walks on the Water
Mt 14.27,29,31

To His disciples in the boat as He walked towards them on the water
Courage! It is I. Don't be afraid!

And then to Peter who wanted to go to meet Him
Come!

And as He reached out to Peter who had started to sink
How little faith you have! Why did you doubt?

The Teaching of the Ancestors
Mt 15.3–9

To the Pharisees and teachers of the Law when they complained that His disciples didn't wash their hands in the proper way before eating
And why do you disobey God's command and follow your own teaching? For God said, 'Respect your father and your mother,' and 'Whoever curses his father or his mother is to be put to death.' But you teach that if a person has something he could use to help his father or mother, but says, 'This belongs to God,' he does not need to honour his father. In this way you disregard God's command, in order to follow your own teaching. You hypocrites! How right Isaiah was when he prophesied about you! 'These people, says God, honour me with their words,
    but their heart is really far away from me.
It is no use for them to worship me,
    because they teach man-made rules as though they were my
        laws!'

The Things That Make a Person Unclean
Mt 15.10–11,13–14,16–20

To the crowds and His disciples as He refuted the teaching of the Pharisees
Listen and understand! It is not what goes into a person's mouth that makes him ritually unclean; rather, what comes out of it makes him unclean.

To His disciples who said the Pharisees were hurt by His words
Every plant which my Father in heaven did not plant will be pulled up. Don't worry about them! They are blind leaders of the blind; and when one blind man leads another, both fall into a ditch.

To Peter who asked Him to explain
You are still no more intelligent than the others. Don't you understand? Anything that goes into a person's mouth goes into his stomach and then on out of his body. But the things that come out of the mouth come from the heart, and these are the things that make a person ritually unclean. For from his heart come the evil ideas which lead him to kill, commit adultery, and do other immoral things; to rob, lie, and slander others. These are the things that make a person unclean. But to eat without washing your hands as they say you should – this doesn't make a person unclean.

A Woman's Faith
Mt 15.24,26,28

To the Canaanite woman who asked him to heal her daughter
I have been sent only to those lost sheep, the people of Israel.

And when she implored Him again
It isn't right to take the children's food and throw it to the dogs

But when she answered that even the dogs ate the leftovers
You are a woman of great faith! What you want will be done for you.

Jesus Feeds Four Thousand Men
Mt 15.32,34

To His disciples concerning feeding another large crowd of people who had been with Him
I feel sorry for these people, because they have been with me for three days and now have nothing to eat. I don't want to send them away without feeding them, for they might faint on their way home.

And when the disciples asked where they would find enough food in the desert to feed all those people
How much bread have you?

The Demand for a Miracle
Mt 16.2–4

To some Pharisees and Sadducees who demanded a miracle
When the sun is setting, you say, 'We are going to have fine weather, because the sky is red.' And early in the morning you say, 'It is going to rain, because the sky is red and dark.' You can predict the weather by looking at the sky, but you cannot interpret the signs concerning these times! How evil and godless are the people of this day! You ask me for a miracle? No! The only miracle you will be given is the miracle of Jonah.

The Yeast of the Pharisees and Sadducees
Mt 16.6,8–11

As a warning to His disciples about the teaching of the Pharisees and Sadducees
Take care; be on your guard against the yeast of the Pharisees and Sadducees.

When they thought He was saying that because they had not brought any bread
Why are you discussing among yourselves about not having any bread? How little faith you have! Don't you understand yet? Don't you remember when I broke the five loaves for the five thousand men? How many baskets did you fill? And what about the seven loaves for the four thousand men? How many baskets did you fill? How is it that you don't understand that I was not

talking to you about bread? Guard yourselves from the yeast of the Pharisees and Sadducees.

Peter's Declaration about Jesus

Mt 16.13,15,17–19

To His disciples
Who do people say the Son of Man is?

When they answered that some said John the Baptist, others Elijah and others Jeremiah or some other prophet
What about you? Who do you say I am?

And to Simon Peter who declared He was the Messiah, the Son of the living God.
Good for you, Simon son of John! For this truth did not come to you from any human being, but it was given to you directly by my Father in heaven. And so I tell you, Peter: you are a rock, and on this rock foundation I will build my church, and not even death will ever be able to overcome it. I will give you the keys of the Kingdom of heaven; what you prohibit on earth will be prohibited in heaven, and what you permit on earth will be permitted in heaven.

Jesus Speaks about His Suffering and Death

Mt 16.21,23,24–28

As He started to speak plainly to His disciples about His suffering
I must go to Jerusalem and suffer much from the elders, the chief priests, and the teachers of the Law. I will be put to death, but three days later I will be raised to life.

When Peter rebuked Him for saying this
Get away from me, Satan! You are an obstacle in my way, because these thoughts of yours don't come from God, but from man.

And then to His disciples again
If anyone wants to come with me, he must forget self, carry his cross, and follow me. For whoever wants to save his own life will lose it; but whoever loses his life for my sake will find it. Will a person gain anything if he wins the whole world but loses his life? Of course not! There is nothing he can give to regain his life. For the Son of Man is about to come in the glory of his Father with his angels, and then he will repay everyone according to his deeds. I assure you that there are some here who will not die until they have seen the Son of Man come as King.

The Transfiguration
Mt 17.7,9,11–12

To Peter, James and John after the Transfiguration when they had heard God's voice
Get up. Don't be afraid!

As they came down the mountain
Don't tell anyone about this vision you have seen until the Son of Man has been raised from death.

And when they asked about Elijah coming first
Elijah is indeed coming first, and he will get everything ready. But I tell you that Elijah has already come and people did not recognize him, but treated him just as they pleased. In the same way they will also ill-treat the Son of Man.

Jesus Heals a Boy with a Demon
Mt 17.17,20

When a man asked Him to help his son who was possessed by an evil spirit which the disciples could not drive out
How unbelieving and wrong you people are! How long must I stay with you? How long do I have to put up with you? Bring the boy here to me!

When His disciples asked Him privately why they had not been able to heal the boy
It was because you haven't enough faith. I assure you that if you have faith as big as a mustard seed, you can say to this hill, 'Go from here to there!' and it will go. You could do anything!

Jesus Speaks Again about His Death
Mt 17.22–23

To His disciples in Galilee concerning His death
The Son of Man is about to be handed over to men who will kill him; but three days later he will be raised to life.

Payment of the Temple-Tax
Mt 17.25, 26–27

To Simon Peter who had been asked whether or not his teacher paid the temple-tax
Simon, what is your opinion? Who pays duties or taxes to the kings of this world? The citizens of the country or the foreigners?

When Peter said the foreigners did
Well, then, that means that the citizens don't have to pay. But we don't want to offend these people. So go to the lake and drop in a line. Pull up the first fish you hook, and in its mouth you will find a coin worth enough for my temple-tax and yours. Take it and pay them our taxes.

Who Is the Greatest?
Mt 18.3–5

To His disciples when they had asked who was the greatest in the Kingdom of heaven
I assure you that unless you change and become like children, you will never enter the Kingdom of heaven. The greatest in the Kingdom of heaven is the one who humbles himself and becomes like this child. And whoever welcomes in my name one such child as this, welcomes me.

Temptations to Sin
Mt 18.6–9

Using a child as an example
If anyone should cause one of these little ones to lose his faith in me, it would be better for that person to have a large millstone tied round his neck and be drowned in the deep sea. How terrible for the world that there are things that make people lose their faith! Such things will always happen – but how terrible for the one who causes them!

If your hand or your foot makes you lose your faith, cut it off and throw it away! It is better for you to enter life without a hand or a foot than to keep both hands and both feet and be thrown into the eternal fire. And if your eye makes you lose your faith, take it out and throw it away! It is better for you to enter life with only one eye than to keep both eyes and be thrown into the fire of hell.

The Parable of the Lost Sheep
Mt 18.10–14

See that you don't despise any of these little ones. Their angels in heaven, I tell you, are always in the presence of my Father in heaven.

What do you think a man does who has a hundred sheep and one of them gets lost? He will leave the other ninety-nine grazing on the hillside and go and look for the lost sheep. When he finds it, I tell you, he feels far happier over this one sheep than over the ninety-nine that did not get lost. In just the same way your Father in heaven does not want any of these little ones to be lost.

A Brother Who Sins
Mt 18.15–17

If your brother sins against you, go to him and show him his fault. But do it privately, just between yourselves. If he listens to you, you have won your brother back. But if he will not listen to you, take one or two other persons with you, so that 'every accusation may be upheld by the testimony of two or more witnesses,' as the scripture says. And if he will not listen to them, then tell the whole thing to the church. Finally, if he will not listen to the church, treat him as though he were a pagan or a tax collector.

Prohibiting and Permitting
Mt 18.18–20

And so I tell all of you: what you prohibit on earth will be prohibited in heaven, and what you permit on earth will be permitted in heaven.

And I tell you more: whenever two of you on earth agree about anything you pray for it, it will be done for you by my Father in heaven. For where two or three come together in my name, I am there with them.

The Parable of the Unforgiving Servant
Mt 18.22–35

To Peter who asked how often he should forgive
No, not seven times, but seventy times seven, because the Kingdom of heaven is like this. Once there was a king who decided to check on his servants' accounts. He had just begun to do so when one of them was brought in who owned him millions of pounds. The servant did not have enough to pay his debt, so the king ordered him to be sold as a slave, with his wife and his children and all that he had, in order to pay the debt. The servant fell on his knees before the king. 'Be patient with me,' he begged, 'and I will pay you everything!' The king felt sorry for him, so he forgave him the debt and let him go.

Then the man went out and met one of his fellow-servants who owed him a few pounds. He grabbed him and started choking him. 'Pay back what you owe me!' he said. His fellow-servant fell down and begged him, 'Be patient with me, and I will pay you back!' But he refused; instead he had him thrown into jail until he should pay the debt. When the other servants saw what had happened, they were very upset and went to the king and told him everything. So he called the servant in. 'You worthless slave!' he said. 'I forgave you the whole amount you owed me, just because you asked me to. You should have had mercy on your fellow-servant, just as I had mercy on you.' The king was very angry, and he sent the servant to jail to be punished until he should pay back the whole amount. That is how my Father in heaven will treat every one of you unless you forgive your brother from your heart.

Jesus Teaches About Divorce
Mt 19.4–6,8–9,11–12

To the Pharisees when they asked if the Jewish law allowed a man to divorce his wife
Haven't you read the scripture that says that in the beginning

the Creator made people male and female? And God said, 'For this reason a man will leave his father and mother and unite with his wife, and the two will become one.' So they are no longer two, but one. Man must not separate, then, what God has joined together.

And when they asked why Moses had permitted a man to hand his wife a divorce notice
Moses gave you permission to divorce your wives because you are so hard to teach. But it was not like that at the time of creation. I tell you, then, that any man who divorces his wife, even though she has not been unfaithful, commits adultery if he marries some other woman.

To His disciples who asked if this meant it would be better not to get married
This teaching does not apply to everyone, but only to those to whom God has given it. For there are different reasons why men cannot marry; some, because they were born that way; others, because men made them that way; and others do not marry for the sake of the Kingdom of heaven. Let him who can accept this teaching do so.

Jesus Blesses Little Children
Mt 19.14

To His disciples when they tried to stop people bringing their children to Him
Let the children come to me and do not stop them, because the Kingdom of heaven belongs to such as these.

The Rich Young Man
Mt 19.18,19,21,23,24,26,28–30

To the man who asked what he should do to receive eternal life
Why do you ask me concerning what is good? There is only One who is good. Keep the commandments if you want to enter life.

When he asked what commandments he should keep
Do not commit murder; do not commit adultery; do not steal; do not accuse anyone falsely; respect your father and your mother; and love your neighbour as you love yourself.

When he said he had obeyed all these commandments and asked what else he need do
If you want to be perfect, go and sell all you have and give the money to the poor, and you will have riches in heaven; then come and follow me.

To His disciples when the young man went away sad, because he was very rich
I assure you: it will be very hard for rich people to enter the Kingdom of heaven. I repeat: it is much harder for a rich person to enter the Kingdom of God than for a camel to go through the eye of a needle.

When the disciples asked in amazement who then could be saved
This is impossible for man, but for God everything is possible.

And when Peter then said that they had left everything to follow Him
You can be sure that when the Son of Man sits on his glorious throne in the New Age, then you twelve followers of mine will also sit on thrones, to rule the twelve tribes of Israel. And everyone who has left houses or brothers or sisters or father or mother or children or fields for my sake, will receive a hundred times more and will be given eternal life. But many who now are first will be last, and many who now are last will be first.

The Workers in the Vineyard
Mt 20.1–16

Underlining His teaching with a parable
The Kingdom of heaven is like this. Once there was a man who went out early in the morning to hire some men to work in his vineyard. He agreed to pay them the regular wage, a silver coin a day, and sent them to work in his vineyard. He went out again to the market place at nine o'clock and saw some men standing there doing nothing, so he told them, 'You also go and work in the vineyard, and I will pay you a fair wage.' So they went. Then at twelve o'clock, and again at three o'clock he did the same thing. It was nearly five o'clock when he went to the market place and saw some other men still standing there. 'Why are you wasting the whole day here doing nothing?' he asked them. 'No one hired us,' they answered. 'Well, then you also go and work in the vineyard,' he told them.

When evening came, the owner told his foreman, 'Call the workers and pay them their wages, starting with those who were hired last and ending with those who were hired first.' The men who had begun to work at five o'clock were paid a silver coin each. So when the men who were the first to be hired came to be paid, they thought they would get more; but they too were given a silver coin each. They took their money and started grumbling against the employer. 'These men who were hired last worked only one hour,' they said, 'while we put up with a whole day's work in the hot sun – yet you paid them the same as you paid us!'

'Listen, friend,' the owner answered one of them. 'I have not cheated you. After all, you agreed to do a day's work for one silver coin. Now take your pay and go home. I want to give this man who was hired last as much as I have given you. Don't I have the right to do as I wish with my own money? Or are you jealous because I am generous?'

So those who are last will be first, and those who are first will be last.

Jesus Speaks a Third Time about His Death
Mt 20.18,19

To His disciples about what would happen in Jerusalem
Listen, we are going up to Jerusalem, where the Son of Man will be handed over to the chief priests and the teachers of the Law. They will condemn him to death and then hand him over to the Gentiles, who will mock him, whip him, and crucify him; but three days later he will be raised to life.

A Mother's Request
Mt 20.21,22,23,25–28

To the wife of Zebedee
What do you want?

And when she asked for a place of honour for her two sons
You don't know what you are asking for.

Then to the sons themselves
Can you drink the cup of suffering that I am about to drink?

When her sons said they could
You will indeed drink from my cup, but I do not have the right to choose who will sit at my right and my left. These places belong to those for whom my Father has prepared them.

And then to the other ten disciples who were angry with the two brothers about this
You know that the rulers of the heathen have power over them, and the leaders have complete authority. This, however, is not the way it shall be among you. If one of you wants to be great, he must be the servant of the rest; and if one of you wants to be first, he must be your slave – like the Son of Man, who did not come to be served, but to serve and to give his life to redeem many people.

Jesus Heals Two Blind Men Mt 20.32	*Before healing two blind men who called out to Him* What do you want me to do for you?
The Triumphant Entry into Jerusalem Mt 21.2,3	*To His disciples as they approached Jerusalem* Go to the village there ahead of you, and at once you will find a donkey tied up with her colt beside her. Untie them and bring them to me. And if anyone says anything, tell him, 'The Master needs them'; and then he will let them go at once.
Jesus Goes to the Temple Mt 21.13,16	*To the money-changers and merchants when He drove them out of the Temple* It is written in the Scriptures that God said, 'My Temple will be called a house of prayer.' But you are making it a hideout for thieves! *When the chief priests and the teachers of the Law heard the people praising Him and angrily asked Him if He heard what they were saying* Indeed I do. Haven't you ever read this scripture? 'You have trained children and babies to offer perfect praise.
Jesus Curses the Fig-Tree Mt 21.19,21–22	*When He was hungry early in the morning and saw a fig-tree without any fruit* You will never again bear fruit! *And then to His disciples after the tree had died* I assure you that if you believe and do not doubt, you will be able to do what I have done to this fig-tree. And not only this, but you will even be able to say to this hill, 'Get up and throw yourself in the sea,' and it will. If you believe, you will receive whatever you ask for in prayer.
The Question about Jesus' Authority Mt 21.24–25,27	*To the chief priests and elders in the Temple when they questioned His authority* I will ask you just one question, and if you give me an answer, I will tell you what right I have to do these things. Where did John's right to baptize come from: was it from God or from man? *And when they would not answer Him for fear of what the people might do* Neither will I tell you, then, by what right I do these things.

The Parable of the Two Sons
Mt 21.28–32

To underline His teaching
Now, what do you think? There was once a man who had two sons. He went to the elder one and said, 'Son, go and work in the vineyard today.' 'I don't want to,' he answered, but later he changed his mind and went. Then the father went to the other son and said the same thing. 'Yes, sir,' he answered, but he did not go. Which one of the two did what his father wanted?

When they said the elder one
I tell you: the tax collectors and the prostitutes are going into the Kingdom of God ahead of you. For John the Baptist came to you showing you the right path to take, and you would not believe him; but the tax collectors and the prostitutes believed him. Even when you saw this, you did not later change your minds and believe him.

The Parable of the Tenants in the Vineyard
Mt 21.33–40,42–43

As He used another parable to teach the people
Listen to another parable. There was once a landowner who planted a vineyard, put a fence around it, dug a hole for the winepress, and built a watch-tower. Then he let out the vineyard to tenants and went on a journey. When the time came to gather the grapes, he sent his slaves to the tenants to receive his share of the harvest. The tenants seized his slaves, beat one, killed another, and stoned another. Again the man sent other slaves, more than the first time, and the tenants treated them the same way. Last of all he sent his son to them. 'Surely they will respect my son,' he said. But when the tenants saw the son, they said to themselves, 'This is the owner's son. Come on, let's kill him, and we will get his property!' So they seized him, threw him out of the vineyard, and killed him.

Now, when the owner of the vineyard comes, what will he do to those tenants?

When they answered that the tenants would be killed and the vineyard let out to others
Haven't you ever read what the Scriptures say?
'The stone which the builders rejected as worthless
    turned out to be the most important of all.
This was done by the Lord;
    what a wonderful sight it is!'
And so I tell you, the Kingdom of God will be taken away from you and given to a people who will produce the proper fruits.

**The Parable
of the Wedding Feast**
Mt 22.2–14

In another parable
The Kingdom of heaven is like this. Once there was a king who prepared a wedding feast for his son. He sent his servants to tell the invited guests to come to the feast, but they did not want to come. So he sent other servants with this message for the guests: 'My feast is ready now; my bullocks and prize calves have been butchered, and everything is ready. Come to the wedding feast!' But the invited guests paid no attention and went about their business: one went to his farm, another to his shop, while others grabbed the servants, beat them, and killed them. The king was very angry, so he sent his soldiers, who killed those murderers and burnt down their city. Then he called his servants and said to them, 'My wedding feast is ready, but the people I invited did not deserve it. Now go to the main streets and invite to the feast as many people as you find. So the servants went out into the streets and gathered all the people they could find, good and bad alike; and the wedding hall was filled with people.

The king went in to look at the guests and saw a man who was not wearing wedding clothes. 'Friend, how did you get in here without wedding clothes?' the king asked him. But the man said nothing. Then the king told the servants, 'Tie him up hand and foot, and throw him outside in the dark. There he will cry and grind his teeth.'

Many are invited, but few are chosen.

**The Question
about Paying Taxes**
Mt 22.18,19,20,21

To the Pharisees when they tried to trap Him by asking whether or not they should pay taxes to the Roman Emperor
You hypocrites! Why are you trying to trap me? Show me the coin for paying the tax!

When they brought Him a coin
Whose face and name are these?

When they said they belonged to the Emperor
Well, then, pay the Emperor what belongs to the Emperor, and pay God what belongs to God.

**The Question
about Rising from Death**
Mt 22.29–32

When the Sadducees, who did not believe that people rose from the dead, asked Him about it
How wrong you are! It is because you don't know the Scriptures or God's power. For when the dead rise to life, they will be like

the angels in heaven and will not marry. Now, as for the dead rising to life: haven't you ever read what God has told you? He said, 'I am the God of Abraham, the God of Isaac, and the God of Jacób.' He is the God of the living, not of the dead.

The Great Commandment
Mt 22.37–40

To a teacher of the Law who asked Him which was the greatest commandment
Love the Lord your God with all your heart, with all your soul, and with all your mind.' This is the greatest and the most important commandment. The second most important commandment is like it: 'Love your neighbour as you love yourself.' The whole Law of Moses and the teachings of the prophets depend on these two commandments.

The Question about the Messiah
Mt 22.42,43–45

To some Pharisees
What do you think about the Messiah? Whose descendant is he?

When they said he was David's descendant
Why, then, did the Spirit inspire David to call him 'Lord'? David said,
'The Lord said to my Lord:
    Sit here on my right
    until I put your enemies under your feet.'
If, then, David called him 'Lord,' how can the Messiah be David's descendant?

Jesus Warns against the Teachers of the Law and the Pharisees
Mt 23.2–12

To the crowds and to His disciples
The teachers of the Law and the Pharisees are the authorized interpreters of Moses' Law. So you must obey and follow everything they tell you to do; do not, however, imitate their actions, because they don't practise what they preach. They tie on to people's backs loads that are heavy and hard to carry, yet they aren't willing even to lift a finger to help them carry those loads. They do everything so that people will see them. Look at the straps with scripture verses on them which they wear on their foreheads and arms, and notice how large they are! Notice also how long are the tassels on their cloaks! They love the best places at feasts and the reserved seats in the synagogues; they love to be greeted with respect in the market-places and to be called 'Teacher.' You must not be called 'Teacher', because you are all brothers of one another and have only one Teacher. And you must not call anyone here on earth 'Father', because you have only the one Father in heaven. Nor should you be called

'Leader', because your one and only leader is the Messiah. The greatest one among you must be your servant. Whoever makes himself great will be humbled, and whoever humbles himself will be made great.

Jesus Condemns Their Hypocrisy
Mt 23.13–28

About the teachers of the Law and the Pharisees
How terrible for you, teachers of the Law and Pharisees! You hypocrites! You lock the door to the Kingdom of heaven in people's faces, and you yourselves don't go in, nor do you allow in those who are trying to enter!

How terrible for you, teachers of the Law and Pharisees! You hypocrites! You sail the seas and cross whole countries to win one convert; and when you succeed, you make him twice as deserving of going to hell as you yourselves are!

How terrible for you, blind guides! You teach, 'If someone swears by the Temple, he isn't bound by his vow; but if he swears by the gold in the Temple, he is bound.' Blind fools! Which is more important, the gold or the Temple which makes the gold holy? You also teach, 'If someone swears by the altar, he isn't bound by his vow; but if he swears by the gift on the altar, he is bound.' How blind you are! Which is the more important, the gift or the altar which makes the gift holy? So then, when a person swears by the altar, he is swearing by it and by all the gifts on it; and when he swears by the Temple, he is swearing by it and by God, who lives there; and when someone swears by heaven, he is swearing by God's throne and by him who sits on it.

How terrible for you, teachers of the Law and Pharisees. You hypocrites! You give to God a tenth even of the seasoning herbs, such as mint, dill, and cumin, but you neglect to obey the really important teachings of the Law, such as justice and mercy and honesty. These you should practise, without neglecting the others. Blind guides! You strain a fly out of your drink, but swallow a camel!

How terrible for you, teachers of the Law and Pharisees! You hypocrites! You clean the outside of your cup and plate, while the inside is full of what you have obtained by violence and selfishness. Blind Pharisee! Clean what is inside the cup first, and then the outside will be clean too!

How terrible for you, teachers of the Law and Pharisees! You hypocrites! You are like whitewashed tombs, which look fine on the outside but are full of bones and decaying corpses on the inside. In the same way, on the outside you appear good to everybody, but inside you are full of hypocrisy and sins.

Jesus Predicts Their Punishment
Mt 23.29–36

How terrible for you, teachers of the Law and Pharisees! You hypocrites! You make fine tombs for the prophets and decorate the monuments of those who lived good lives; and you claim that if you had lived during the time of your ancestors, you would not have done what they did and killed the prophets. So you actually admit that you are the descendants of those who murdered the prophets! Go on, then, and finish what your ancestors started! You snakes and sons of snakes! How do you expect to escape from being condemned to hell? And so I tell you that I will send you prophets and wise men and teachers; you will kill some of them, crucify others, and whip others in the synagogues and chase them from town to town. As a result, the punishment for the murder of all innocent men will fall on you, from the murder of innocent Abel to the murder of Zachariah son of Berachiah, whom you murdered between the Temple and the altar. I tell you, indeed: the punishment for all these murders will fall on the people of this day!

Jesus' Love for Jerusalem
Mt 23.37–39

Jerusalem, Jerusalem! You kill the prophets and stone the messengers God has sent you! How many times have I wanted to put my arms round all your people, just as a hen gathers her chicks under her wings, but you would not let me! And so your Temple will be abandoned and empty. From now on, I tell you, you will never see me again until you say, 'God bless him who comes in the name of the Lord.'

Jesus Speaks of the Destruction of the Temple
Mt 24.2

When His disciples drew His attention to the buildings of the Temple
Yes, you may well look at all these. I tell you this: not a single stone here will be left in its place; every one of them will be thrown down.

Troubles and Persecutions
Mt 24.4–14

To the disciples who asked Him in private how they would know when all this was about to happen
Be on your guard, and do not let anyone deceive you. Many men, claiming to speak for me, will come and say, 'I am the Messiah!' and they will deceive many people. You are going to hear the noise of battles close by and the news of battles far

away; but do not be troubled. Such things must happen, but they do not mean that the end has come. Countries will fight each other, kingdoms will attack one another. There will be famines and earthquakes everywhere. All these things are like the first pains of childbirth.

Then you will be arrested and handed over to be punished and be put to death. All mankind will hate you because of me. Many will give up their faith at that time; they will betray one another and hate one another. Then many false prophets will appear and deceive many people. Such will be the spread of evil that many people's love will grow cold. But whoever holds out to the end will be saved. And this Good News about the Kingdom will be preached through all the world for a witness to all mankind; and then the end will come.

The Awful Horror
Mt 24.15–28

You will see 'The Awful Horror' of which the prophet Daniel spoke. It will be standing in the holy place. Then those who are in Judaea must run away to the hills. A man who is on the roof of his house must not take the time to go down and get his belongings from the house. A man who is in the field must not go back to get his cloak. How terrible it will be in those days for women who are pregnant and for mothers with little babies! Pray to God that you will not have to run away during the winter or on a Sabbath! For the trouble at that time will be far more terrible than any there has ever been, from the beginning of the world to this very day. Nor will there ever be anything like it again. But God has already reduced the number of days; had he not done so, nobody would survive. For the sake of his chosen people, however, God will reduce the days.

Then, if anyone says to you, 'Look, here is the Messiah!' or 'There he is!' – do not believe him. For false Messiahs and false prophets will appear; they will perform great miracles and wonders in order to deceive even God's chosen people, if possible. Listen! I have told you this before the time comes.

Or, if people should tell you, 'Look, he is out in the desert!' – don't go there; or if they say, 'Look, he is hiding here!' – don't believe it. For the Son of Man will come like the lightning which flashes across the whole sky from the east to the west.

Wherever there is a dead body, the vultures will gather.

**The Coming
of the Son of Man**
Mt 24.29–31

Soon after the trouble of those days, the sun will grow dark, the moon will no longer shine, the stars will fall from heaven, and the powers in space will be driven from their courses. Then the sign of the Son of Man will appear in the sky; and all the peoples on earth will weep as they see the Son of Man coming on the clouds of heaven with power and great glory. The great trumpet will sound, and he will send out his angels to the four corners of the earth, and they will gather his chosen people from one end of the world to the other.

The Lesson of the Fig-Tree
Mt 24.32–35

In a series of parables about the coming of the Son of Man
Let the fig-tree teach you a lesson. When its branches become green and tender and it starts putting out leaves, you know that summer is near. In the same way, when you see all these things, you will know that the time is near, ready to begin. Remember that all these things will happen before the people now living have all died. Heaven and earth will pass away, but my words will never pass away.

**No One Knows
the Day and Hour**
Mt 24.36–44

No one knows, however, when that day and hour will come – neither the angels in heaven nor the Son; the Father alone knows. The coming of the Son of Man will be like what happened in the time of Noah. In the days before the flood people ate and drank, men and women married, up to the very day Noah went into the boat; yet they did not realize what was happening until the flood came and swept them all away. That is how it will be when the Son of Man comes. At that time two men will be working in a field: one will be taken away, the other will be left behind. Two women will be at a mill grinding meal: one will be taken away, the other will be left behind.

Be on your guard, then, because you do not know what day your Lord will come. If the owner of a house knew the time when the thief would come, you can be sure that he would stay awake and not let the thief break into his house. So then, you also must always be ready, because the Son of Man will come at an hour when you are not expecting him.

**The Faithful
or the Unfaithful Servant**
Mt 24.45–51

Who, then, is a faithful and wise servant? He is the one that his master has placed in charge of the other servants to give them their food at the proper time. How happy that servant is if his master finds him doing this when he comes home! Indeed, I tell you, the master will put that servant in charge of all his property. But if he is a bad servant, he will tell himself that his master will not come back for a long time, and he will begin to beat his fellow-servants and to eat and drink with drunkards. Then that servant's master will come back one day when the servant does not expect him and at a time he does not know. The master will cut him in pieces and make him share the fate of the hypocrites. There he will cry and grind his teeth.

The Parable of the Ten Girls
Mt 25.1–13

At that time the Kingdom of heaven will be like this. Once there were ten girls who took their oil lamps and went out to meet the bridegroom. Five of them were foolish, and the other five were wise. The foolish ones took their lamps but did not take any extra oil with them, while the wise ones took containers full of oil for their lamps. The bridegroom was late in coming, so the girls began to nod and fall asleep.

It was already midnight when the cry rang out, 'Here is the bridegroom! Come and meet him!' The ten girls woke up and trimmed their lamps. Then the foolish ones said to the wise ones, 'Let us have some of your oil, because our lamps are going out.' 'No, indeed,' the wise ones answered, 'there is not enough for you and for us. Go to the shop and buy some for yourselves.' So the foolish girls went off to buy some oil; and while they were gone, the bridegroom arrived. The five girls who were ready went in with him to the wedding feast, and the door was closed.

Later the other girls arrived. 'Sir, sir! Let us in!' they cried out. 'Certainly not! I don't know you,' the bridegroom answered.

Be on your guard, then, because you do not know the day or the hour.

The Parable of the Three Servants
Mt 25.14–30

At that time the Kingdom of heaven will be like this. Once there was a man who was about to go on a journey; he called his servants and put them in charge of his property. He gave to each one according to his ability: to one he gave five thousand silver coins, to another he gave two thousand, and to another he gave one thousand. Then he left on his journey. The servant who had received five thousand coins went at once and invested his money and earned another five thousand. In the same way the servant who had received two thousand coins earned another two thousand. But the servant who had received one thousand coins went off, dug a hole in the ground, and hid his master's money.

After a long time the master of those servants came back and settled accounts with them. The servant who had received five thousand coins came in and handed over the other five thousand. 'You gave me five thousand coins, sir,' he said. 'Look! Here are another five thousand that I have earned.' 'Well done, you good and faithful servant!' said his master. 'You have been faithful in managing small amounts, so I will put you in charge of large amounts. Come on in and share my happiness!'

Then the servant who had been given two thousand coins came in and said, 'You gave me two thousand coins, sir. Look! Here are another two thousand that I have earned.' 'Well done, you good and faithful servant!' said his master. 'You have been faithful in managing small amounts, so I will put you in charge of large amounts. Come on in and share my happiness!'

Then the servant who had received one thousand coins came in and said, 'Sir, I know you are a hard man; you reap harvests where you did not sow, and you gather crops where you did not scatter seed. I was afraid, so I went off and hid your money in the ground. Look! Here is what belongs to you.'

'You bad and lazy servant!' his master said. 'You knew, did you, that I reap harvests where I did not sow and gather crops where I did not scatter seed? Well, then, you should have deposited my money in the bank, and I would have received it all back with interest when I returned. Now, take the money away from him and give it back to the one who has ten thousand coins. For to every person who has something, even more will be given, and he will have more than enough; but the person who has nothing, even the little that he has will be taken away from him. As for this useless servant – throw him outside in the darkness; there he will cry and grind his teeth.'

The Final Judgement
Mt 25.31–46

When the Son of Man comes as King and all the angels with him, he will sit on his royal throne, and the people of all the nations will be gathered before him. Then he will divide them into two groups, just as a shepherd separates the sheep from the goats. He will put the righteous people on his right and the others on his left. Then the King will say to the people on his right, 'Come, you that are blessed by my Father! Come and possess the kingdom which has been prepared for you ever since the creation of the world. I was hungry and you fed me, thirsty and you gave me a drink; I was a stranger and you received me in your homes, naked and you clothed me; I was sick and you took care of me, in prison and you visited me.'

The righteous will then answer him, 'When, Lord, did we ever see you hungry and feed you, or thirsty and give you a drink? When did we ever see you a stranger and welcome you in our homes, or naked and clothe you? When did we ever see you sick or in prison, and visit you?' The King will reply, 'I tell you, whenever you did this for one of the least important of these brothers of mine, you did it for me!'

Then he will say to those on his left, 'Away from me, you that are under God's curse! Away to the eternal fire which has been prepared for the Devil and his angels! I was hungry but you would not feed me, thirsty but you would not give me a drink; I was a stranger but you would not welcome me in your homes, naked but you would not clothe me; I was sick and in prison but you would not take care of me.'

Then they will answer him, 'When Lord, did we ever see you hungry or thirsty or a stranger or naked or sick or in prison, and would not help you?' The King will reply, 'I tell you, whenever you refused to help one of these least important ones, you refused to help me.' These, then, will be sent off to eternal punishment, but the righteous will go to eternal life.

The Plot against Jesus
Mt 26.2

To His disciples after He had finished teaching
In two days, as you know, it will be the Passover Festival, and the Son of Man will be handed over to be crucified.

Jesus is Anointed at Bethany
Mt 26.10–13

To His disciples who complained when a woman anointed Him with an expensive perfume.
Why are you bothering this woman? It is a fine and beautiful thing that she has done for me. You will always have poor people with you, but you will not always have me. What she did was to pour this perfume on my body to get me ready for burial. Now, I assure you that wherever this gospel is preached all over the world, what she has done will be told in memory of her.

Jesus Eats the Passover Meal with His Disciples
Mt 26.18,21,23–24,25

As He sent His disciples to get the Passover meal ready
Go to a certain man in the city, and tell him: 'The Teacher says, My hour has come; my disciples and I will celebrate the Passover at your house.'

To His disciples during the Passover meal
I tell you, one of you will betray me.

And when the disciples were upset and began to question Him
One who dips his bread in the dish with me will betray me. The Son of Man will die as the Scriptures say he will, but how terrible for that man who betrays the Son of Man! It would have been better for that man if he had never been born!

To Judas who asked if He meant him
So you say.

The Lord's Supper
Mt 26.26,27–29

While they were eating, as He took a piece of bread, gave a prayer of thanks, broke it, and gave it to His disciples
Take and eat it; this is my body.

Then when He took a cup, gave thanks to God, and gave it to them
Drink it, all of you; this is my blood, which seals God's covenant, my blood poured out for many for the forgiveness of sins. I tell you, I will never again drink this wine until the day I drink the new wine with you in my Father's Kingdom.

Jesus Predicts Peter's Denial
Mt 26.31,32,34

To His disciples
This very night all of you will run away and leave me, for the scripture says, 'God will kill the shepherd, and the sheep of the flock will be scattered.' But after I am raised to life, I will go to Galilee ahead of you.

When Peter said he would never leave Him even though the others did
I tell you that before the cock crows tonight, you will say three times that you do not know me.

Jesus Prays in Gethsemane
Mt 26.36,38,39,40–41,42,45–46

To His disciples when they had gone with Him to Gethsemane
Sit here while I go over there and pray.

In grief and anguish to Peter and the two sons of Zebedee whom He took with Him
The sorrow in my heart is so great that it almost crushes me. Stay here and keep watch with me.

A little further on as He threw Himself on the ground and prayed
My Father, if it is possible, take this cup of suffering from me!
Yet not what I want, but what you want.

When He returned to the three disciples and found them asleep
How is it that you three were not able to keep watch with me
even for one hour? Keep watch and pray that you will not fall
into temptation. The spirit is willing, but the flesh is weak.

As He went away and prayed a second time
My Father, if this cup of suffering cannot be taken away unless I
drink it, your will be done.

When He returned to the three disciples after He had prayed for a third time
Are you still sleeping and resting? Look! The hour has come for
the Son of Man to be handed over to the power of sinful men.
Get up, let us go. Look, here is the man who is betraying me!

The Arrest of Jesus
Mt 26.50,52–54,55–56

When one of His disciples, Judas, escorted by a large armed crowd, came up to Him and kissed Him
Be quick about it, friend!

And when someone tried to defend Him at His arrest, by striking at the High Priest's slave and cutting off his ear
Put your sword back in its place. All who take the sword will die
by the sword. Don't you know that I could call on my Father for
help, and at once he would send me more than twelve armies of
angels? But in that case, how could the Scriptures come true
which say that this is what must happen.

To the crowd
Did you have to come with swords and clubs to capture me, as
though I were an outlaw? Every day I sat down and taught in
the Temple, and you did not arrest me. But all this has
happened in order to make what the prophets wrote in the
Scriptures come true.

Jesus Before the Council
Mt 26.64.

Before the Council, when Caiaphas, the High Priest, asked Him if He was the Messiah, the Son of God
So you say. But I tell all of you: from this time on you will see
the Son of Man sitting on the right of the Almighty and coming
on the clouds of heaven!

Pilate Questions Jesus
Mt 27.11

When He was brought before the Roman Governor who then asked Him if
He was the King of the Jews
So you say.

The Death of Jesus
Mt 27.46

As He hung on the cross after having been sentenced to death
Eli, Eli, lema sabachthani? . . . My God, my God, why did you
abandon me?

The Resurrection
Mt 28.9.10

To Mary Magdalene and the other Mary, on the Sunday after His death,
when they found His tomb empty, and were returning with joy to tell the
other disciples that He had risen from the dead
Peace be with you.

When they came up to Him and worshipped Him
Do not be afraid. Go and tell my brothers to go to Galilee, and
there they will see me.

Jesus Appears
to His Disciples
Mt 28.18–20

To His eleven disciples after His Resurrection
I have been given all authority in heaven and on earth. Go,
then, to all peoples everywhere and make them my disciples:
baptize them in the name of the Father, the Son, and the Holy
Spirit, and teach them to obey everything I have commanded
you. And I will be with you always, to the end of the age.

Christ's Words

in Mark

Christ's Words in Mark

Jesus Calls Four Fishermen
Mk 1.15,17

As He began to preach the Good News in Galilee
The right time has come, and the Kingdom of God is near! Turn away from your sins and believe the Good News!

When He called Simon and Andrew
Come with me, and I will teach you to catch men.

A Man with an Evil Spirit
Mk 1.25

When a man with an evil spirit entered the synagogue at Capernaum
Be quiet, and come out of the man!

Jesus Preaches in Galilee
Mk 1.38

To Simon and his companions next morning when they found Him outside the town in a lonely place
We must go on to the other villages round here. I have to preach in them also, because that is why I came.

Jesus Heals a Man
Mk 1.41,44

When a man with a dreaded skin-disease told Him He could make him clean if He wanted to
I do want to. Be clean!

And when the man was healed at once
Listen, don't tell anyone about this. But go straight to the priest and let him examine you; then in order to prove to everyone that you are cured, offer the sacrifice that Moses ordered.

Jesus Heals a Paralysed Man
Mk 2.5,8–10,11

As He healed a paralysed man
My son, your sins are forgiven.

To some teachers of the Law who then accused Him of blasphemy
Why do you think such things? Is it easier to say to this paralysed man, 'Your sins are forgiven', or to say, 'Get up, pick up your mat, and walk'? I will prove to you, then, that the Son of Man has authority on earth to forgive sins.

And to the man again
I tell you, get up, pick up your mat, and go home!

Jesus Calls Levi
Mk 2.14,17

As He called Levi, a tax collector
Follow me.

To some Pharisees who asked why He ate with tax collectors and other outcasts
People who are well do not need a doctor, but only those who are sick. I have not come to call respectable people, but outcasts.

The Question about Fasting
Mk 2.19–22

To the followers of John the Baptist when they asked why His disciples did not fast
Do you expect the guests at a wedding party to go without food? Of course not! As long as the bridegroom is with them, they will not do that. But the day will come when the bridegroom will be taken away from them, and then they will fast.

No one uses a piece of new cloth to patch up an old coat, because the new patch will shrink and tear off some of the old cloth, making an even bigger hole. Nor does anyone pour new wine into used wineskins, because the wine will burst the skins, and both the wine and the skins will be ruined. Instead, new wine must be poured into fresh wineskins.

The Question about the Sabbath
Mk 2.25–28

To the Pharisees who asked why His disciples were picking ears of corn on the Sabbath
Have you never read what David did that time when he needed something to eat? He and his men were hungry, so he went into the house of God and ate the bread offered to God. This happened when Abiathar was the High Priest. According to our Law only the priests may eat this bread – but David ate it and even gave it to his men.

The Sabbath was made for the good of man; man was not made for the Sabbath. So the Son of Man is Lord even of the Sabbath.

The Man with a Paralysed Hand
Mk 3.3,4,5

To the man with a paralysed hand
Come up here to the front.

And to the Pharisees concerning healing on the Sabbath
What does our Law allow us to do on the Sabbath? To help or to harm? To save a man's life or to destroy it?

And to the man
Stretch out your hand.

Jesus Chooses the Twelve Apostles
Mk 3.14–15

To the twelve apostles just after He had chosen them
I have chosen you to be with me. I will also send you out to preach, and you will have authority to drive out demons.

Jesus and Beelzebul
Mk 3.23–29

To some teachers of the Law who accused Him of healing through the power of Beelzebul
How can Satan drive out Satan? If a country divides itself into groups which fight each other, that country will fall apart. If a family divides itself into groups which fight each other, that family will fall apart. So if Satan's kingdom divides into groups, it cannot last, but will fall apart and come to an end.

No one can break into a strong man's house and take away his belongings unless he first ties up the strong man; then he can plunder his house.

I assure you that people can be forgiven all their sins and all the evil things they may say. But whoever says evil things against the Holy Spirit will never be forgiven, because he has committed an eternal sin.

Jesus' Mother and Brothers
Mk 3.33,34–35

When He was told that His mother and brothers were outside wanting to see Him
Who is my mother? Who are my brothers?

And as He looked at the people sitting round Him
Look! Here are my mother and my brothers! Whoever does what God wants him to do is my brother, my sister, my mother.

The Parable of the Sower
Mk 4.3–9

To the people as He told them parables by the lake-side
Listen! Once there was a man who went out to sow corn. As he scattered the seed in the field some of it fell along the path, and the birds came and ate it up. Some of it fell on rocky ground, where there was little soil. The seeds soon sprouted, because the soil wasn't deep. Then, when the sun came up, it burnt the young plants; and because the roots had not grown deep enough, the plants soon dried up. Some of the seed fell among thorn bushes, which grew up and choked the plants, and they didn't produce any corn. But some seeds fell in good soil, and the plants sprouted, grew, and produced corn: some had thirty grains, others sixty, and others a hundred. Listen, then, if you have ears!

The Purpose of the Parables
Mk 4.11–12

To those who came with the twelve disciples to ask Him to explain the parables
You have been given the secret of the Kingdom of God. But the others, who are on the outside, hear all things by means of parables, so that,
'They may look and look,
    yet not see;
they may listen and listen,
    yet not understand,
For if they did, they would turn to God,
    and he would forgive them.

Jesus Explains the Parable of the Sower
Mk 4.13–20

To His followers to help them to understand
Don't you understand this parable? How, then, will you ever understand any parable? The sower sows God's message. Some people are like the seeds that fall along the path; as soon as they hear the message, Satan comes and takes it away. Other people are like the seeds that fall on rocky ground. As soon as they hear the message they receive it gladly. But it does not sink deep into them, and they don't last long. So when trouble or persecution comes because of the message, they give up at once. Other people are like the seeds sown among the thorn bushes. These are the ones who hear the message, but the worries about this life, the love for riches, and all other kinds of desires crowd in and choke the message, and they don't bear fruit. But other people are like the seeds sown in good soil. They hear the message, accept it, and bear fruit: some thirty, some sixty, and some a hundred.

A Lamp under a Bowl
Mk 4.21–25

To His disciples
Does anyone ever bring in a lamp and put it under a bowl or under the bed? Doesn't he put it on a lampstand? Whatever is hidden away will be brought out into the open, and whatever is covered up will be uncovered. Listen, then, if you have ears!

Pay attention to what you hear! The same rules you use to judge others will be used by God to judge you – but with even greater severity. The person who has something will be given more, and the person who has nothing will have taken away from him even the little he has.

The Parable of the Growing Seed
Mk 4.26–29

As He continued to teach them about the Kingdom of God
The Kingdom of God is like this. A man scatters seed in his field. He sleeps at night, is up and about during the day, and all the while the seeds are sprouting and growing. Yet he does not know how it happens. The soil itself makes the plants grow and bear fruit; first the tender stalk appears, then the ear, and finally the ear full of corn. When the corn is ripe, the man starts cutting it with his sickle, because harvest time has come.

The Parable of the Mustard Seed
Mk 4.30–32

What shall we say the Kingdom of God is like? What parable shall we use to explain it? It is like this. A man takes a mustard seed, the smallest seed in the world, and plants it in the ground. After a while it grows up and becomes the biggest of all plants. It puts out such large branches that the birds come and make their nests in its shade.

Jesus Calms a Storm
Mk 4.35,39,40

To His disciples
Let us go across to the other side of the lake.

To the wind during a storm which blew up while He and the disciples were in the boat
Be quiet!

And to the waves
Be still!

And then to His disciples
Why are you frightened? Have you still no faith?

Jesus Heals a Man with Evil Spirits
Mk 5.8,9,19

As He commanded the evil spirit that possessed the man at Gerasa
Evil spirit, come out of this man!

Then as He questioned him
What is your name?

When the man, who was now in his right mind, wanted to go with Him
Go back home to your family and tell them how much the Lord has done for you and how kind he has been to you.

Jairus' Daughter and the Woman Who Touched Jesus' Cloak
Mk 5.30,34,36,39,41,43

By the lakeside, when a woman in the crowd who had suffered from severe bleeding for twelve years touched the edge of His cloak, hoping to be healed
Who touched my clothes?

And to the woman, who, realizing she had been healed, threw herself at His feet
My daughter, your faith has made you well. Go in peace, and be healed of your trouble.

To Jairus, when He heard that his twelve year old daughter had just died
Don't be afraid, only believe.

To the people in Jairus' house
Why all this confusion? Why are you crying? The child is not dead – she is only sleeping!

To the child
Talitha, koum . . . Little girl, I tell you to get up!

And to those around her
Give her something to eat.

Jesus Is Rejected at Nazareth
Mk 6.4

In the synagogue at Nazareth, His home town, when He taught the people and was rejected by them
A prophet is respected everywhere except in his own home town and by his relatives and his family.

Jesus Sends out the Twelve Disciples
Mk 6.8–11

To His disciples as He sent them out two by two to preach, teach and heal
Don't take anything with you on your journey except a stick – no bread, no beggar's bag, no money in your pockets. Wear sandals, but don't carry an extra shirt. Wherever you are welcomed, stay in the same house until you leave that place. If you come to a town where people do not welcome you or will not listen to you, leave it and shake the dust off your feet. That will be a warning to them!

Jesus Feeds Five Thousand Men
Mk 6.31,37,38

To the Twelve when they returned
Let us go off by ourselves to some place where we will be alone and you can rest for a while.

When His disciples showed concern for the large crowd who had followed them and listened to His teaching
You yourselves give them something to eat.

And when they asked if they were to go and spend two hundred silver coins on bread in order to do so
How much bread have you got? Go and see.

Jesus Walks on the Water
Mk 6.50

To His disciples in the boat as He walked towards them on the water
Courage! It is I. Don't be afraid!

The Teaching of the Ancestors
Mk 7.6–13

To the Pharisees and teachers of the Law who asked why His disciples ate with ritually unclean hands
How right Isaiah was when he prophesied about you! You are hypocrites, just as he wrote:
'These people, says God, honour me with their words,
    but their heart is really far away from me.
It is no use for them to worship me,
    because they teach man-made rules
    as though they were God's laws!'
You put aside God's command and obey the teachings of men. You have a clever way of rejecting God's law in order to uphold your own teaching. For Moses commanded, 'Respect your father and your mother,' and, 'Whoever curses his father or his mother is to be put to death.' But you teach that if a person has something he could use to help his father or mother, but says, 'This is Corban' (which means, it belongs to God), he is excused from helping his father or mother. In this way the teaching you pass on to others cancels out the word of God. And there are many other things like this that you do.

The Things that Make a Person Unclean
Mk 7.14–15,18–19,20–23

To the crowd as He refuted the teaching of the Pharisees
Listen to me, all of you, and understand. There is nothing that goes into a person from the outside which can make him ritually unclean. Rather, it is what comes out of a person that makes him unclean.

And to His disciples
You are no more intelligent than the others. Don't you understand? Nothing that goes into a person from the outside can really make him unclean, because it does not go into his heart but into his stomach and then goes on out of the body.

And when He had thus declared that all foods were fit to be eaten
It is what comes out of a person that makes him unclean. For from the inside, from a person's heart, come the evil ideas which lead him to do immoral things, to rob, kill, commit adultery, be greedy, and do all sorts of evil things; deceit, indecency, jealousy, slander, pride and folly – all these evil things come from inside a person and make him unclean.

A Woman's Faith
Mk 7.27,29

To the Canaanite woman who asked Him to heal her daughter
Let us first feed the children. It isn't right to take the children's food and throw it to the dogs.

And when she answered that even the dogs ate the children's leftovers
Because of that answer, go back home, where you will find that the demon has gone out of your daughter!

Jesus Heals a Deaf-Mute
Mk 7.34

To a man who was deaf and could hardly speak, as He healed him
Ephphatha . . . Open up!

Jesus Feeds Four Thousand People
Mk 8.2–3,5

To His disciples concerning feeding another large crowd of people
I feel sorry for these people, because they have been with me for three days and now have nothing to eat. If I send them home without feeding them, they will faint as they go, because some of them have come a long way.

And when they asked where they could find enough food for all those people in the desert
How much bread have you got?

The Pharisees Ask for a Miracle
Mk 8.12

To some Pharisees who demanded a miracle
Why do the people of this day ask for a miracle? No, I tell you! No such proof will be given to these people!

The Yeast of the Pharisees and of Herod
Mk 8.15,17–19,20,21

To the disciples who had forgotten to bring enough bread
Take care, and be on your guard against the yeast of the Pharisees and the yeast of Herod.

When they thought He was saying that because they did not have any bread
Why are you discussing about not having any bread? Don't you know or understand yet? Are your minds so dull? You have eyes – can't you see? You have ears – can't you hear? Don't you remember when I broke the five loaves for the five thousand people? How many baskets full of leftover pieces did you take up?

When they said, 'Twelve'
And when I broke the seven loaves for the four thousand people, how many baskets full of leftover pieces did you take up?

And when they said, 'Seven'
And you still don't understand?

**Jesus Heals
a Blind Man at Bethsaida**
Mk 8.23,26

To a blind man after He had placed His hands on him
Can you see anything?

To the man again when He sent him home, healed
Don't go back into the village.

**Peter's Declaration
about Jesus**
Mk 8.27,29,30

To His disciples
Tell me, who do people say I am?

When they answered that some said John the Baptist, others Elijah and others one of the prophets
What about you? Who do you say I am?

And when Simon Peter declared He was the Messiah
Do not tell anyone about me.

**Jesus Speaks
about His Suffering
and Death**
Mk 8.31,33,34—9.1

As He started to speak plainly to His disciples about His suffering and death
The Son of Man must suffer much and be rejected by the elders, the chief priests, and the teachers of the Law. He will be put to death, but three days later he will rise to life.

When Peter rebuked Him for saying this
Get away from me, Satan. Your thoughts don't come from God but from man!

And then to the crowd and to His disciples again
If anyone wants to come with me, he must forget self, carry his cross, and follow me. For whoever wants to save his own life will lose it; but whoever loses his life for me and for the gospel will save it. Does a person gain anything if he wins the whole world but loses his life? Of course not! There is nothing he can give to regain his life. If a person is ashamed of me and of my teaching in this godless and wicked day, then the Son of Man will be ashamed of him when he comes in the glory of his Father with the holy angels.

I tell you, there are some here who will not die until they have seen the Kingdom of God come with power.

The Transfiguration
Mk 9.9,12–13

To Peter, James and John as they were coming down the mountain after the Transfiguration
Don't tell anyone what you have seen, until the Son of Man has risen from death.

And when they asked about Elijah coming first
Elijah is indeed coming first in order to get everything ready. Yet why do the Scriptures say that the Son of Man will suffer much and be rejected? I tell you, however, that Elijah has already come and that people treated him just as they pleased, as the Scriptures say about him.

Jesus Heals a Boy with an Evil Spirit
Mk 9.16,19,21,23,25,29

To the rest of His disciples when He found them with a large crowd around them
What are you arguing with them about?

When He heard that the disciples had not been able to cast out an evil spirit which had possessed a boy
How unbelieving you people are! How long must I stay with you? How long do I have to put up with you? Bring the boy to me!

To the father when the spirit threw the boy into a fit
How long has he been like this?

And when the father asked Him to help if He possibly could
Yes, if you yourself can! Everything is possible for the person who has faith.

To the evil spirit
Deaf and dumb spirit, I order you to come out of the boy and never go into him again!

And later when His disciples asked Him privately why they had not been able to drive the spirit out
Only prayer can drive this kind out; nothing else can.

Jesus Speaks Again about His Death
Mk 9.31

To His disciples in Galilee concerning His death
The Son of Man will be handed over to men who will kill him. Three days later, however, he will rise to life.

Who Is the Greatest?
Mk 9.33,35,37

To His disciples when they had been arguing amongst themselves about who was the greatest
What were you arguing about on the road?

When they would not answer Him
Whoever wants to be first must place himself last of all and be the servant of all.

And with His arms round a child
Whoever welcomes in my name one of these children, welcomes me; and whoever welcomes me, welcomes not only me but also the one who sent me.

Whoever
Is Not against Us
Is For Us
Mk 9.39–41

To John, who had tried to stop a man who was not a disciple from driving out demons in His name
Do not try to stop him, because no one who performs a miracle in my name will be able soon afterwards to say evil things about me. For whoever is not against us is for us. I assure you that anyone who gives you a drink of water because you belong to me will certainly receive his reward.

Temptations to Sin
Mk 9.42–50

If anyone should cause one of these little ones to lose his faith in me, it would be better for that person to have a large millstone tied round his neck and be thrown into the sea. So if your hand makes you lose your faith, cut it off! It is better for you to enter life without a hand than to keep both hands and go off to hell, to the fire that never goes out. And if your foot makes you lose your faith, cut it off! It is better for you to enter life without a foot than to keep both feet and be thrown into hell. And if your eye makes you lose your faith, take it out! It is better for you to enter the Kingdom of God with only one eye than to keep both eyes and be thrown into hell. There 'the worms that eat them never die, and the fire that burns them is never put out.'

Everyone will be purified by fire as a sacrifice is purified by salt.

Salt is good; but if it loses its saltiness, how can you make it salty again?

Have the salt of friendship among yourselves, and live in peace with one another.

Jesus Teaches about Divorce
Mk 10.3,5–9,11–12

To the Pharisees when they asked if the Jewish law allowed a man to divorce his wife
What law did Moses give you?

And when they said that Moses had given permission for a man to write a divorce notice
Moses wrote this law for you because you are so hard to teach. But in the beginning, at the time of creation, 'God made them male and female,' as the scripture says. 'And for this reason a

man will leave his father and mother and unite with his wife, and the two will become one.' So they are no longer two, but one. Man must not separate, then, what God has joined together.

To the disciples who asked Him afterwards about this matter
A man who divorces his wife and marries another woman commits adultery against his wife. In the same way, a woman who divorces her husband and marries another man commits adultery.

Jesus Blesses Little Children
Mk 10.14–15

To His disciples when they tried to stop people bringing their children to Him
Let the children come to me and do not stop them because the Kingdom of God belongs to such as these. I assure you that whoever does not receive the Kingdom of God like a child will never enter it.

The Rich Man
Mk 10.18–19,21,23,
24–25,27,29–31

To the man who asked Him what he should do to receive eternal life
Why do you call me good? No one is good except God alone. You know the commandments: 'Do not commit murder; do not commit adultery; do not steal; do not accuse anyone falsely; do not cheat; respect your father and your mother.'

When the man said he had obeyed all these commandments since he was young
You need only one thing. Go and sell all you have and give the money to the poor, and you will have riches in heaven; then come and follow me.

To His disciples when the man went away sad, because he was very rich
How hard it will be for rich people to enter the Kingdom of God!

When the disciples were shocked at these words
My children, how hard it is to enter the Kingdom of God! It is much harder for a rich person to enter the Kingdom of God than for a camel to go through the eye of a needle.

When the disciples asked in amazement who could in fact be saved
This is impossible for man, but not for God; everything is possible for God.

And when Peter then said that they had left everything to follow Him
Yes, and I tell you that anyone who leaves home or brothers or sisters or mother or father or children or fields for me and for the gospel, will receive much more in this present age. He will receive a hundred times more houses, brothers, sisters, mothers, children and fields – and persecutions as well; and in the age to come he will receive eternal life. But many who now are first will be last, and many who now are last will be first.

Jesus Speaks a Third Time about His Death
Mk 10.33–34

To His disciples, on their way to Jerusalem, concerning His death
Listen, we are going up to Jerusalem where the Son of Man will be handed over to the chief priests and the teachers of the Law. They will condemn him to death and then hand him over to the Gentiles, who will mock him, spit on him, whip him, and kill him; but three days later he will rise to life.

The Request of James and John
Mk 10.36,38,39–40,42–45

When James and John came to ask Him to do something for them
What is it?

And when they asked to be given a place of honour in His Kingdom
You don't know what you are asking for. Can you drink the cup of suffering that I must drink? Can you be baptized in the way I must be baptized?

When they said they could
You will indeed drink the cup I must drink and be baptized in the way I must be baptized. But I do not have the right to choose who will sit at my right and my left. It is God who will give these places to those for whom he has prepared them.

And to the other ten disciples, who were angry when they heard about this
You know that the men who are considered rulers of the heathen have power over them, and the leaders have complete authority. This, however, is not the way it is among you. If one of you wants to be great, he must be the servant of the rest; and if one of you wants to be first, he must be the slave of all. For even the Son of Man did not come to be served; he came to serve and to give his life to redeem many people.

Jesus Heals Blind Bartimaeus
Mk 10.49,51,52

When a blind beggar named Bartimaeus called out to Him as He passed by
Call him.

When he came
What do you want me to do for you?

When he said he wanted to see again
Go, your faith has made you well.

The Triumphant Entry into Jerusalem
Mk 11.2–3

To two of His disciples as they approached Jerusalem
Go to the village there ahead of you. As soon as you get there, you will find a colt tied up that has never been ridden. Untie it and bring it here. And if someone asks you why you are doing that, tell him that the Master needs it and will send it back at once.

Jesus Curses the Fig-Tree
Mk 11.14

The next day when He felt hungry and saw a fig-tree without any fruit
No one shall ever eat figs from you again!

Jesus Goes to the Temple
Mk 11.17

To the people after driving the money-changers and merchants out of the Temple
It is written in the Scriptures that God said, 'My Temple will be called a house of prayer for the people of all nations.' But you have turned it into a hideout for thieves!

The Lesson from the Fig-Tree
Mk 11.22–25

The following morning when His disciples saw that the fig-tree had now died
Have faith in God. I assure you that whoever tells this hill to get up and throw itself in the sea and does not doubt in his heart, but believes that what he says will happen, it will be done for him. For this reason I tell you: When you pray and ask for something, believe that you have received it, and you will be given whatever you ask for. And when you stand and pray, forgive anything you may have against anyone, so that your Father in heaven will forgive the wrongs you have done.

The Question about Jesus' Authority
Mk 11.29–30,33

To the chief priests, teachers of the Law and elders in the Temple when they questioned His authority
I will ask you just one question, and if you give me an answer, I will tell you what right I have to do these things. Tell me, where did John's right to baptize come from: was it from God or from man?

And when they would not answer for fear of what the people might do
Neither will I tell you, then, by what right I do these things.

The Parable of the Tenants in the Vineyard
Mk 12.1–11

As He spoke to them in parables
Once there was a man who planted a vineyard, put a fence round it, dug a hole for the winepress, and built a watch-tower. Then he let out the vineyard to tenants and left home on a journey. When the time came to gather the grapes, he sent a slave to the tenants to receive from them his share of the harvest. The tenants seized the slave, beat him, and sent him back without a thing. Then the owner sent another slave; the tenants beat him over the head and treated him shamefully. The owner sent another slave and they killed him: and they treated many others the same way, beating some and killing others. The only one left to send was the man's own dear son. Last of all, then, he sent his son to the tenants. 'I am sure they will respect my son,' he said. But those tenants said to one another, 'This is the owner's son. Come on, let's kill him, and his property will be ours!' So they seized the son and killed him and threw his body out of the vineyard.

What then, will the owner of the vineyard do? He will come and kill those men and hand the vineyard over to other tenants. Surely you have read this scripture?

'The stone which the builders rejected as worthless
    turned out to be the most important of all.
This was done by the Lord;
    what a wonderful sight it is!'

The Question about Paying Taxes
Mk 12.15,16,17

To some Pharisees and members of Herod's party when they tried to trap Him by asking whether or not they should pay taxes to the Roman Emperor
Why are you trying to trap me? Bring a silver coin, and let me see it.

When they brought Him a coin
Whose face and name are these?

When they said they were the Emperor's
Well, then, pay the Emperor what belongs to the Emperor, and pay God what belongs to God.

The Question about Rising from Death
Mk 12.24–27

When the Sadducees, who did not believe that people rose from the dead, asked Him about it
How wrong you are! And do you know why? It is because you

don't know the Scriptures or God's power. For when the dead rise to life, they will be like the angels in heaven and will not marry. Now, as for the dead being raised: haven't you ever read in the Book of Moses the passage about the burning bush? There it is written that God said to Moses, 'I am the God of Abraham, the God of Isaac, and the God of Jacob.' He is the God of the living, not the dead. You are completely wrong!

The Great Commandment
Mk 12.29–31,34

To a teacher of the Law who asked Him which was the most important commandment
The most important one is this: 'Listen, Israel! The Lord our God is the only Lord. Love the Lord your God with all your heart, with all your soul, with all your mind, and with all your strength.' The second most important commandment is this: 'Love your neighbour as you love yourself.' There is no other commandment more important then these two.

And when the man wholeheartedly agreed with Him
You are not far from the Kingdom of God.

The Question about the Messiah
Mk 12.35–37

As He was teaching in the Temple
How can the teachers of the Law say that the Messiah will be the descendant of David? The Holy Spirit inspired David to say: 'The Lord said to my Lord:
    Sit here on my right
    until I put your enemies under your feet.'
David himself called him 'Lord'; so how can the Messiah be David's descendant?

Jesus Warns against the Teachers of the Law
Mk 12.38–40

As a large crowd listened to Him gladly
Watch out for the teachers of the Law, who like to walk around in their long robes and be greeted with respect in the marketplace, who choose the reserved seats in the synagogues and the best places at feasts. They take advantage of widows and rob them of their homes, and then make a show of saying long prayers. Their punishment will be all the worse!

The Widow's Offering
Mk 12.43–44

To His disciples when He saw a poor widow dropping two small coins worth about a penny in the temple treasury
I tell you that this poor widow put more in the offering box than all the others. For the others put in what they had to spare of their riches; but she, poor as she is, put in all she had – she gave all she had to live on.

**Jesus Speaks
of the Destruction
of the Temple**
Mk 13.2

As one of His disciples exclaimed how wonderful the Temple buildings were
You see these great buildings? Not a single stone here will be left in its place; every one of them will be thrown down.

Troubles and Persecutions
Mk 13.5–13

To Peter, James, John, and Andrew who asked Him in private how they would know when all these things were about to happen
Be on guard, and don't let anyone deceive you. Many men, claiming to speak for me, will come and say, 'I am he!' and they will deceive many people. And don't be troubled when you hear the noise of battles close by and news of battles far away. Such things must happen, but they do not mean that the end has come. Countries will fight each other; kingdoms will attack one another, there will be earthquakes everywhere, and there will be famines. These things are like the first pains of childbirth.

You yourselves must be on guard. You will be arrested and taken to court. You will be beaten in the synagogues; you will stand before rulers and kings for my sake to tell them the Good News. But before the end comes, the gospel must be preached to all peoples. And when you are arrested and taken to court, do not worry beforehand about what you are going to say; when the time comes, say whatever is then given to you. For the words you speak will not be yours; they will come from the Holy Spirit. Men will hand over their own brothers to be put to death, and fathers will do the same to their children. Children will turn against their parents and have them put to death. Everyone will hate you because of me. But whoever holds out to the end will be saved.

The Awful Horror
Mk 13.14–23

You will see 'The Awful Horror' standing in the place where he should not be . . . Then those who are in Judaea must run away to the hills. A man who is on the roof of his house must not lose time by going down into the house to get anything to take with him. A man who is in the field must not go back to the house for his cloak. How terrible it will be in those days for women who are pregnant and for mothers with little babies! Pray to God that these things will not happen in the winter! For the trouble of those days will be far worse than any the world has ever known from the very beginning when God created the world until the present time. Nor will there ever be anything like it again. But the Lord has reduced the number of those days; if he had not, nobody would survive. For the sake of his chosen people, however, he has reduced those days.

Then, if anyone says to you, 'Look, here is the Messiah!' or, 'Look, there he is!' – do not believe him. For false Messiahs and false prophets will appear. They will perform miracles and wonders in order to deceive even God's chosen people, if possible. Be on your guard! I have told you everything before the time comes.

The Coming of the Son of Man
Mk 13.24–27

In the days after that time of trouble the sun will grow dark, the moon will no longer shine, the stars will fall from heaven, and the powers in space will be driven from their courses. Then the Son of Man will appear, coming in the clouds with great power and glory. He will send the angels out to the four corners of the earth to gather God's chosen people from one end of the world to the other.

The Lesson of the Fig-Tree
Mk 13.28–31

Let the fig-tree teach you a lesson. When its branches become green and tender and it starts putting out leaves, you know that summer is near. In the same way, when you see these things happening, you will know that the time is near, ready to begin. Remember that all these things will happen before the people now living have all died. Heaven and earth will pass away, but my words will never pass away.

No One Knows the Day or Hour
Mk 13.32–37

No one knows, however, when that day or hour will come – neither the angels in heaven, nor the Son; only the Father knows. Be on watch, be alert, for you do not know when the time will come. It will be like a man who goes away from home on a journey and leaves his servants in charge, after giving to each one his own work to do and after telling the doorkeeper to keep watch. Be on guard, then, because you do not know when the master of the house is coming – it might be in the evening or at midnight or before dawn or at sunrise. If he comes suddenly, he must not find you asleep. What I say to you, then, I say to all: Watch!

Jesus Is Anointed at Bethany
Mk 14.6–9

To some people who complained when a woman anointed Him with an expensive perfume
Leave her alone! Why are you bothering her? She has done a fine and beautiful thing for me. You will always have poor people with you, and any time you want to, you can help them.

But you will not always have me. She did what she could; she poured perfume on my body to prepare it ahead of time for burial. Now, I assure you that wherever the gospel is preached all over the world, what she has done will be told in memory of her.

Jesus Eats the Passover Meal with His Disciples
Mk 14.13–15,18,20–21

When He sent two of His disciples to get the Passover meal ready
Go into the city, and a man carrying a jar of water will meet you. Follow him to the house he enters, and say to the owner of the house: 'The Teacher says, Where is the room where my disciples and I will eat the Passover meal?' Then he will show you a large upstairs room, prepared and furnished, where you will get everything ready for us.

To His disciples during the Passover meal
I tell you that one of you will betray me – one who is eating with me.

And when His disciples were upset and began to question Him
It will be one of you twelve, one who dips his bread in the dish with me. The Son of Man will die as the Scriptures say he will; but how terrible for that man who betrays the Son of Man! It would have been better for that man if he had never been born!

The Lord's Supper
Mk 14.22,24–25

While they were eating, as He took a piece of bread, gave a prayer of thanks, broke it, and gave it to His disciples
Take it, this is my body.

Then, when He took a cup, gave thanks to God, and handed it to them, and they all drank from it
This is my blood which is poured out for many, my blood which seals God's covenant. I tell you, I will never again drink this wine until the day I drink the new wine in the Kingdom of God.

Jesus Predicts Peter's Denial
Mk 14.27–28,30

To His disciples
All of you will run away and leave me, for the scripture says, 'God will kill the shepherd, and the sheep will all be scattered.' But after I am raised to life, I will go to Galilee ahead of you.

When Peter said he would never leave Him even though the others did
I tell you that before the cock crows twice tonight, you will say three times that you do not know me.

Jesus Prays in Gethsemane
Mk 14.32,34,36,37–38,41–42

When He and His disciples had gone to Gethsemane
Sit here while I pray.

In distress and anguish to Peter, James, and John whom He took with Him
The sorrow in my heart is so great that it almost crushes me. Stay here and keep watch.

A little farther on as He threw Himself on the ground and prayed
Father, my Father! All things are possible for you. Take this cup of suffering away from me. Yet not what I want, but what you want.

To Peter when He returned and found the three disciples asleep
Simon, are you asleep? Weren't you able to stay awake even for one hour? Keep watch, and pray that you will not fall into temptation. The spirit is willing, but the flesh is weak.

After going away and praying twice more, and returning each time to find His disciples asleep
Are you still sleeping and resting? Enough! The hour has come! Look, the Son of Man is now being handed over to the power of sinful men. Get up, let us go. Look, here is the man who is betraying me!

The Arrest of Jesus
Mk 14.48–49

To the crowd who came to arrest Him, after Judas, one of the twelve disciples, had betrayed Him with a kiss
Did you have to come with swords and clubs to capture me, as though I were an outlaw? Day after day I was with you teaching in the Temple, and you did not arrest me. But the Scriptures must come true.

Jesus Before the Council
Mk 14.62

Before the Council when the High Priest asked Him if He was the Messiah, the Son of the Blessed God
I am, and you will all see the Son of Man seated on the right of the Almighty and coming with the clouds of heaven!

Peter Denies Jesus
Mk 14.72

As recalled by Peter when he heard the cock crow
Before the cock crows twice you will say three times that you do not know me.

Jesus is Brought before Pilate Mk 15.2	*When He was brought before Pilate who asked Him if He was the King of the Jews* So you say.
The Death of Jesus Mk 15.34	*As He hung on the cross after having been sentenced to death* Eloi, Eloi, lema sabachthani? . . . My God, my God, why did you abandon me?
Jesus Appears to the Eleven Mk 16.15–18	*When He appeared to His eleven disciples after His death and resurrection, and having scolded them for not believing those who had seen Him alive* Go throughout the whole world and preach the gospel to all mankind. Whoever believes and is baptized will be saved; whoever does not believe will be condemned. Believers will be given the power to perform miracles; they will drive out demons in my name; they will speak in strange tongues; if they pick up snakes or drink poison, they will not be harmed; they will place their hands on sick people, who will get well.

Christ's Words

in Luke

Christ's Words in Luke

The Boy Jesus in the Temple
Lk 2.49

At the age of twelve, when His parents found Him in the Temple in Jerusalem, talking to the Jewish leaders
Why did you have to look for me? Didn't you know that I had to be in my Father's house?

The Temptation of Jesus
Lk 4.4,8,12

As He was being tempted by the Devil to turn stones into bread
The Scripture says, 'Man cannot live on bread alone.'

To worship Satan
The scripture says, 'Worship the Lord your God and serve only him!'

And to throw Himself down from the Temple
The scripture says, 'Do not put the Lord your God to the test.'

Jesus Is Rejected at Nazareth
Lk 4.18–19,21,23–27

In the synagogue at Nazareth, His home town, when He read from the book of the prophet Isaiah
The Spirit of the Lord is upon me,
    because he has chosen me to bring good news to the poor.
He has sent me to proclaim liberty to the captives
    and recovery of sight to the blind;
to set free the oppressed
    and announce that the time has come
    when the Lord will save his people.

After He had finished reading
This passage of scripture has come true today, as you heard it being read.

When the people marvelled because He was only the son of Joseph
I am sure that you will quote this proverb to me, 'Doctor, heal yourself.' You will also tell me to do here in my home town the same things you heard were done in Capernaum. I tell you this, a prophet is never welcomed in his home town.

Listen to me: it is true that there were many widows in Israel during the time of Elijah, when there was no rain for three and a half years and a severe famine spread throughout the whole land. Yet Elijah was not sent to anyone in Israel, but only to a widow living in Zarephath in the territory of Sidon. And there were many people suffering from a dreaded skin-disease who lived in Israel during the time of the prophet Elisha; yet not one of them was healed, but only Naaman the Syrian.

A Man with an Evil Spirit
Lk 4.35

In the synagogue at Capernaum, to a man with an evil spirit
Be quiet and come out of the man!

Jesus Preaches in the Synagogues
Lk 4.43

The following day, when the people of the town looked for Him and tried to keep Him from leaving
I must preach the Good News of the Kingdom of God in other towns also, because that is what God sent me to do.

Jesus Calls the First Disciples
Lk 5.4,10

To Simon, after He had sat in his boat and taught from it
Push the boat out further to the deep water, and you and your partners let down your nets for a catch.

Again to Simon, when he and the others were amazed at the large number of fish they had caught
Don't be afraid; from now on you will be catching men.

Jesus Heals a Man
Lk 5.13,14

When a man with a dreaded skin-disease told Him He could make him clean if He wanted to
I do want to. Be clean!

And when he was healed at once
Don't tell anyone, but go straight to the priest and let him examine you; then to prove to everyone that you are cured, offer the sacrifice as Moses ordered.

Jesus Heals a Paralysed Man
Lk 5.20,22–24

As He healed a paralysed man
Your sins are forgiven, my friend.

To the teachers of the Law and the Pharisees who then began to accuse Him of blasphemy
Why do you think such things? Is it easier to say, 'Your sins are forgiven you,' or to say, 'Get up and walk'? I will prove to you, then, that the Son of Man has authority on earth to forgive sins.

And to the man again
I tell you, get up, pick up your bed, and go home!

Jesus Calls Levi
Lk 5.27,31–32

When He called Levi, a tax collector
Follow me.

And to some Pharisees and teachers of the Law who asked why Jesus ate with tax collectors
People who are well do not need a doctor, but only those who are sick. I have not come to call respectable people to repent, but outcasts.

The Question about Fasting
Lk 5.34–35,36–39

To some people who asked why His disciples didn't fast, when the disciples of John fasted frequently, as did the disciples of the Pharisees
Do you think you can make the guests at a wedding party go without food as long as the bridegroom is with them? Of course not! But the day will come when the bridegroom will be taken away from them, and then they will fast.

And when He told this parable
No one tears a piece off a new coat to patch up an old coat. If he does, he will have torn the new coat, and the piece of new cloth will not match the old. Nor does anyone pour new wine into used wineskins, because the new wine will burst the skins, the wine will pour out and the skins will be ruined. Instead, new wine must be poured into fresh wineskins! And no one wants new wine after drinking old wine. 'The old is better,' he says.

The Question about the Sabbath
Lk 6.3–5

To the Pharisees, when His disciples picked ears of corn and ate the grain on the Sabbath
Haven't you read what David did when he and his men were hungry? He went into the house of God, took the bread offered to God, ate it, and gave it also to his men. Yet it is against our Law for anyone except the priests to eat that bread.

The Son of Man is Lord of the Sabbath.

The Man with a Paralysed Hand
Lk 6.8,9,10

To a man with a paralysed hand
Stand up and come here to the front.

And to the Pharisees concerning healing the man on the Sabbath
I ask you: What does our Law allow us to do on the Sabbath? To help or to harm? To save a man's life or destroy it?

And to the man
Stretch out your hand.

Happiness and Sorrow
Lk 6.20–26

As He taught His disciples and the crowds
Happy are you poor;
   the Kingdom of God is yours!
Happy are you who are hungry now;
   you will be filled!
Happy are you who weep now;
   you will laugh!
Happy are you when people hate you, reject you, insult you, and say that you are evil, all because of the Son of Man! Be glad when that happens, and dance for joy, because a great reward is kept for you in heaven. For their ancestors did the very same things to the prophets.
But how terrible for you who are rich now;
   you have had your easy life!
How terrible for you who are full now;
   you will go hungry!
How terrible for you who laugh now;
   you will mourn and weep!
How terrible when all people speak well of you; their ancestors said the very same things about the false prophets.

Love for Enemies
Lk 6.27–36

But I tell you who hear me: Love your enemies, do good to those who hate you, bless those who curse you, and pray for those who ill-treat you. If anyone hits you on one cheek, let him hit the other one too; if someone takes your coat, let him have your shirt as well. Give to everyone who asks you for something, and when someone takes what is yours, do not ask for it back. Do for others just what you want them to do for you.

If you love only the people who love you, why should you receive a blessing? Even sinners love those who love them! And if you do good only to those who do good to you, why should you receive a blessing? Even sinners do that! And if you lend only to those from whom you hope to get it back, why should you receive a blessing? Even sinners lend to sinners, to get back the same amount! No! Love your enemies and do good to them; lend and expect nothing back. You will then have a great reward, and you will be sons of the Most High God. For he is good to the ungrateful and the wicked. Be merciful just as your Father is merciful.

Judging Others
Lk 6.37–38,39–42

Do not judge others, and God will not judge you; do not condemn others and God will not condemn you; forgive others, and God will forgive you. Give to others, and God will give to you. Indeed, you will receive a full measure, a generous helping, poured into your hands – all that you can hold. The measure you use for others is the one that God will use for you.

And as He told them a parable
One blind man cannot lead another one; if he does, both will fall into a ditch. No pupil is greater than his teacher; but every pupil, when he has completed his training, will be like his teacher.

Why do you look at the speck in your brother's eye, but pay no attention to the log in your own eye? How can you say to your brother, 'Please, brother, let me take that speck out of your eye,' yet cannot even see the log in your own eye? You hypocrite! First take the log out of your own eye, and then you will be able to see clearly to take the speck out of your brother's eye.

A Tree and Its Fruit
Lk 6.43–45

A healthy tree does not bear bad fruit, nor does a poor tree bear good fruit. Every tree is known by the fruit it bears; you do not pick figs from thorn bushes or gather grapes from bramble bushes. A good person brings good out of the treasure of good things in his heart; a bad person brings bad out of his treasure of bad things. For the mouth speaks what the heart is full of.

The Two House Builders
Lk 6.46–49

Why do you call me, 'Lord, Lord,' and yet don't do what I tell you? Anyone who comes to me and listens to my words and obeys them – I will show you what he is like. He is like a man who, in building his house, dug deep and laid the foundation on rock. The river overflowed and hit that house but could not shake it, because it was well built. But anyone who hears my words and does not obey them is like a man who built his house without laying a foundation; when the flood hit that house it fell at once – and what a terrible crash that was!

Jesus Heals a Roman Officer's Servant
Lk 7.9

To the crowd concerning a Roman officer who had sent asking Him to heal his servant
I tell you, I have never found faith like this, not even in Israel!

Jesus Raises a Widow's Son
Lk 7.13,14

To a widow at her son's funeral
Don't cry.

And when He had walked over to the coffin
Young man! Get up, I tell you!

**The Messengers
from John the Baptist**
Lk 7.22–23,24–28,31–35

*To John's disciples when they asked Him if He was the one John said was
going to come, or if they were to expect someone else*
Go back and tell John what you have seen and heard: the blind
can see, the lame can walk, those who suffer from dreaded skin-
diseases are made clean, the deaf can hear, the dead are raised
to life, and the Good News is preached to the poor. How happy
are those who have no doubts about me!

And to the crowds about John the Baptist
When you went out to John in the desert, what did you expect
to see? A blade of grass bending in the wind? What did you go
out to see? A man dressed up in fancy clothes? People who dress
like that and live in luxury are found in palaces! Tell me, what
did you go out to see? A prophet? Yes indeed, but you saw much
more than a prophet. For John is the one of whom the scripture
says: 'God said, I will send my messenger ahead of you to open
the way for you.' I tell you, John is greater than any man who
has ever lived. But he who is least in the Kingdom of God is
greater than John.

About the people's reaction to John
Now to what can I compare the people of this day? What are
they like? They are like children sitting in the market-place. One
group shouts to the other, 'We played wedding music for you,
but you wouldn't dance! We sang funeral songs but you
wouldn't cry!' John the Baptist came, and he fasted and drank
no wine, and you said, 'He has a demon in him!' The Son of
Man came, and he ate and drank, and you said, 'Look at this
man! He is a glutton and a drinker, a friend of tax collectors and
other outcasts!' God's wisdom, however, is shown to be true by
all who accept it.

**Jesus at the Home
of Simon the Pharisee**
Lk 7.40,41–42,43–47,48,50

*When a known sinful woman had anointed His feet with a costly perfume,
and His host, Simon, disapproved*
Simon, I have something to tell you.

Then as Simon listened
There were two men who owed money to a moneylender. One
owed him five hundred silver coins, and the other one fifty.

Neither of them could pay him back, so he cancelled the debts of both. Which one, then, will love him more?

And when Simon answered that it would be the one who was forgiven more
You are right. Do you see this woman? I came into your home, and you gave me no water for my feet, but she has washed my feet with her tears and dried them with her hair. You did not welcome me with a kiss, but she has not stopped kissing my feet since I came. You provided no olive-oil for my head, but she has covered my feet with perfume. I tell you, then, the great love she has shown proves that her many sins have been forgiven. But whoever has been forgiven little shows only a little love.

To the woman
Your sins are forgiven.

And to the woman again when the others began to question this
Your faith has saved you; go in peace.

The Parable of the Sower
Lk 8.5–8

To the people as He told them parables
Once there was a man who went out to sow corn. As he scattered the seed in the field, some of it fell along the path, where it was stepped on, and the birds ate it up. Some of it fell on rocky ground, and when the plants sprouted, they dried up because the soil had no moisture. Some of the seed fell among thorn bushes, which grew up with the plants and choked them. And some seeds fell in good soil; the plants grew and produced corn, a hundred grains each. Listen, then, if you have ears!

The Purpose of the Parables
Lk 8.10

To the disciples who asked Him what this parable meant
The knowledge of the secrets of the Kingdom of God has been given to you, but to the rest it comes by means of parables, so that they may look but not see, and listen but not understand.

Jesus Explains the Parable of the Sower
Lk 8.11–5

This is what the parable means: the seed is the word of God. The seeds that fell along the path stand for those who hear; but the Devil comes and takes the message away from their hearts in order to keep them from believing and being saved. The seeds that fell on rocky ground stand for those who hear the message and receive it gladly. But it does not sink deep into them; they believe only for a while but when the time of testing comes, they fall away. The seeds that fell among thorn bushes stand for those who hear; but the worries and riches and pleasures of this life crowd in and choke them, and their fruit never ripens. The seeds that fell in good soil stand for those who hear the message and retain it in a good and obedient heart, and they persist until they bear fruit.

A Lamp under a Bowl
Lk 8.16–18

No one lights a lamp and covers it with a bowl or puts it under a bed. Instead, he puts it on the lampstand, so that people will see the light as they come in.

Whatever is hidden away will be brought out into the open, and whatever is covered up will be found and brought to light.

Be careful, then, how you listen; because whoever has something will be given more, but whoever has nothing will have taken away from him even the little he thinks he has.

Jesus' Mother and Brothers
Lk 8.21

When He was told that His mother and brothers were standing outside wanting to see Him
My mother and brothers are those who hear the word of God and obey it.

Jesus Calms a Storm
Lk 8.22,25

As He got into a boat with His disciples
Let us go across to the other side of the lake.

To His disciples after calming a storm
Where is your faith?

Jesus Heals a Man with Demons
Lk 8.30,39

To the evil spirit that possessed a man at Gerasa
What is your name?

When the man, who was now in his right mind, wanted to go with Him
Go back home and tell what God has done for you.

Jairus' Daughter and the Woman Who Touched Jesus' Cloak
Lk 8.45,46,48,50,52,54

When a sick woman came through the crowd to touch the edge of His cloak, believing that she would be healed
Who touched me?

When Peter said that everyone was crowding in on Him
Someone touched me, for I knew it when power went out of me.

And to the woman who, realizing she had been healed, threw herself at His feet
My daughter, your faith has made you well. Go in peace.

After Jairus had been told that his twelve year old daughter had just died
Don't be afraid; only believe, and she will be well.

To the people in Jairus' house
Don't cry; the child is not dead – she is only sleeping!

And to the child
Get up, my child!

Jesus Sends Out the Twelve Disciples
Lk 9.3–5

To the twelve disciples as He sent them out to preach, teach and heal
Take nothing with you for the journey: no stick, no beggar's bag, no food, no money, not even an extra shirt. Wherever you are welcomed, stay in the same house until you leave that town; wherever people don't welcome you, leave that town and shake the dust off your feet as a warning to them.

Jesus Feeds Five Thousand Men
Lk 9.13,14

When His disciples showed concern for a large, hungry crowd which had followed Him all day as He taught and healed
You yourselves give them something to eat.

When the disciples said they had only five loaves and two fish
Make the people sit down in groups of about fifty each.

Peter's Declaration about Jesus
Lk 9.18,20

To His disciples
Who do the crowds say I am?

When they answered that some said John the Baptist, others Elijah, others one of the prophets come back to life
What about you? Who do you say I am?

Jesus Speaks about His Suffering and Death
Lk 9.22,23–27

As He ordered the disciples to secrecy after Peter had declared Him to be the Messiah
The Son of Man must suffer much and be rejected by the elders, the chief priests, and the teachers of the Law. He will be put to death, but three days later he will be raised to life.

If anyone wants to come with me, he must forget self, take up his cross every day, and follow me. For whoever wants to save his own life will lose it, but whoever loses his life for my sake will save it. Will a person gain anything if he wins the whole world but is himself lost or defeated? Of course not! If a person is ashamed of me and of my teaching, then the Son of Man will be ashamed of him when he comes in his glory and in the glory of the Father and of the holy angels. I assure you that there are some here who will not die until they have seen the Kingdom of God.

Jesus Heals a Boy with an Evil Spirit
Lk 9.41

After the disciples had been unable to cast out an evil spirit
How unbelieving and wrong you people are! How long must I stay with you? How long do I have to put up with you?

Then to the man whose son was possessed
Bring your son here.

Jesus Speaks Again about His Death
Lk 9.44

To His disciples concerning His death
Don't forget what I am about to tell you! The Son of Man is going to be handed over to the power of men.

Who Is the Greatest?
Lk 9.48

To His disciples when, after an argument amongst themselves about who was the greatest, He stood a child by His side
Whoever welcomes this child in my name, welcomes me; and whoever welcomes me, also welcomes the one who sent me. For he who is least among you all is the greatest.

Whoever Is Not against You Is for You
Lk 9.50

To John and the other disciples who had tried to stop a man who was not a disciple from driving out demons in Jesus' name
Do not try to stop him, because whoever is not against you is for you.

The Would-be Followers of Jesus
Lk 9.58,60,62

To a man who wanted to follow Him
Foxes have holes, and birds have nests, but the Son of Man has nowhere to lie down and rest.

To another man who wanted first to bury his father
Let the dead bury their own dead. You go and proclaim the Kingdom of God.

And to another who wanted first to say goodbye to his family
Anyone who starts to plough and then keeps looking back is of no use to the Kingdom of God.

Jesus Sends Out the Seventy-two
Lk 10.2–12

When He instructed the seventy-two men He sent ahead of Him, two by two, to the places He intended to visit
There is a large harvest, but few workers to gather it in. Pray to the owner of the harvest that he will send out workers to gather in his harvest. Go! I am sending you like lambs among wolves.

Don't take a purse or a beggar's bag or shoes; don't stop to greet anyone on the road. Whenever you go into a house, first say, 'Peace be with this house.' If a peace-loving man lives there, let your greeting of peace remain on him; if not, take back your greeting of peace. Stay in that same house, eating and drinking whatever they offer you, for a worker should be given his pay. Don't move round from one house to another. Whenever you go into a town and are made welcome, eat what is set before you, heal the sick in that town, and say to the people there, 'The Kingdom of God has come near you.' But whenever you go into a town and are not welcomed, go out in the streets and say, 'Even the dust from your town that sticks to our feet we wipe off against you. But remember that the Kingdom of God has come near you!' I assure you that on Judgement Day God will show more mercy to Sodom than to that town!

The Unbelieving Towns
Lk 10.13–15,16

About the people who did not believe in Him
How terrible it will be for you, Chorazin! How terrible for you too, Bethsaida! If the miracles which were performed in you had been performed in Tyre and Sidon, the people there would long ago have sat down, put on sackcloth, and sprinkled ashes on themselves, to show that they had turned from their sins! God will show more mercy on Judgement Day to Tyre and Sidon than to you. And as for you, Capernaum! Did you want to lift yourself up to heaven? You will be thrown down to hell!

And to His disciples
Whoever listens to you listens to me; whoever rejects you rejects me; and whoever rejects me rejects the one who sent me.

The Return of the Seventy-two
Lk 10.18–20

After the seventy-two had returned in great joy because even the evil spirits had obeyed them when commanded in Jesus' name
I saw Satan fall like lightning from heaven. Listen! I have given you authority, so that you can walk on snakes and scorpions and overcome all the power of the Enemy, and nothing will hurt you. But don't be glad because the evil spirits obey you; rather be glad because your names are written in heaven.

Jesus Rejoices
Lk 10.21–22,23–24

When He was filled with joy by the Holy Spirit
Father, Lord of heaven and earth! I thank you because you have shown to the unlearned what you have hidden from the wise and learned. Yes, Father, this was how you wanted it to happen.

My Father has given me all things. No one knows who the Son is except the Father, and no one knows who the Father is except the Son and those to whom the Son chooses to reveal him.

And to His disciples privately
How fortunate you are to see the things you see! I tell you that many prophets and kings wanted to see what you see, but they could not, and to hear what you hear, but they did not.

The Parable of the Good Samaritan
Lk 10.26,28,30–35,36,37

To a teacher of the Law who asked Him what he should do to receive eternal life
What do the Scriptures say? How do you interpret them?

When the man answered that they said to love God and your neighbour
You are right. Do this and you will live.

To show the man who his neighbour was
There was once a man who was going down from Jerusalem to Jericho when robbers attacked him, stripped him, and beat him up, leaving him half dead. It so happened that a priest was going down that road; but when he saw the man, he walked on by, on the other side. In the same way a Levite also came along, went over and looked at the man, and then walked on by, on the other side. But a Samaritan who was travelling that way came upon the man, and when he saw him, his heart was filled with pity. He went over to him, poured oil and wine on his wounds and bandaged them; then he put the man on his own animal and took him to an inn, where he took care of him. The next day he took out two silver coins and gave them to the innkeeper. 'Take care of him,' he told the innkeeper, 'and when I come back this way, I will pay you whatever else you spend on him.'

In your opinion, which one of these three acted like a neighbour towards the man attacked by the robbers?

And when the teacher of the Law answered that it was the one who was kind to him
You go, then, and do the same.

Jesus Visits Martha and Mary
Lk 10.41,42

To Martha who was upset when her sister, Mary, listened to the Lord's teaching, instead of helping her
Martha, Martha! You are worried and troubled over so many things, but just one is needed. Mary has chosen the right thing, and it will not be taken away from her.

Jesus' Teaching on Prayer
Lk 11.2–13

One day when Jesus' disciples asked Him to teach them to pray
When you pray, say this:

'Father:
    May your holy name be honoured;
    may your Kingdom come.
    Give us day by day the food we need.
    Forgive us our sins,
      for we forgive everyone who does us wrong.
    And do not bring us to hard testing.'

Suppose one of you should go to a friend's house at midnight and say to him, 'Friend, let me borrow three loaves of bread. A friend of mine who is on a journey has just come to my house, and I haven't got any food for him!' And suppose your friend should answer from inside, 'Don't bother me! The door is already locked, and my children and I are in bed. I can't get up and give you anything.' Well, what then? I tell you that even if he will not get up and give you the bread because you are his friend, yet he will get up and give you everything you need because you are not ashamed to keep on asking.

And so I say to you: Ask, and you will receive; seek, and you will find; knock, and the door will be opened to you. For everyone who asks will receive, and he who seeks will find, and the door will be opened to anyone who knocks. Would any of you who are fathers give your son a snake when he asks for fish? Or would you give him a scorpion when he asks for an egg? Bad as you are, you know how to give good things to your children. How much more, then, will the Father in heaven give the Holy Spirit to those who ask him!

Jesus and Beelzebul
Lk 11.17–23

To those who said He drove out demons through the power of Beelzebul
Any country that divides itself into groups which fight each other will not last very long; a family divided against itself falls apart. So if Satan's kingdom has groups fighting each other, how can it last? You say that I drive out demons because Beelzebul gives me the power to do so. If this is how I drive them out, how do your followers drive them out? Your own followers prove that you are wrong! No, it is rather by means of God's power that I drive out demons, and this proves that the Kingdom of God has already come to you.

When a strong man, with all his weapons ready, guards his own house, all his belongings are safe. But when a stronger man attacks him and defeats him, he carries away all the weapons the owner was depending on and divides up what he stole.

Anyone who is not for me is really against me; anyone who does not help me gather is really scattering.

The Return of the Evil Spirit
Lk 11.24–26

When an evil spirit goes out of a person, it travels over dry country looking for a place to rest. If it can't find one, it says to itself, 'I will go back to my house.' So it goes back and finds the house clean and tidy. Then it goes out and brings seven other spirits even worse than itself, and they come and live there. So when it is all over, that person is in a worse state than he was at the beginning.

True Happiness
Lk 11.28

When a woman from the crowd called His mother happy
Rather, how happy are those who hear the word of God and obey it!

The Demand for a Miracle
Lk 11.29–32

To the people as they crowded round Him
How evil are the people of this day! They ask for a miracle, but none will be given them except the miracle of Jonah. In the same way that the prophet Jonah was a sign for the people of Nineveh, so the Son of Man will be a sign for the people of this day. On Judgement Day the Queen of Sheba will stand up and accuse the people of today, because she travelled all the way from her country to listen to King Solomon's wise teaching; and I tell you there is something here greater than Solomon. On Judgement Day the people of Nineveh will stand up and accuse you, because they turned from their sins when they heard Jonah preach; and I assure you that there is something here greater than Jonah!

The Light of the Body
Lk 11.33–36

No one lights a lamp and then hides it or puts it under a bowl; instead, he puts it on the lampstand, so that people may see the light as they come in. Your eyes are like a lamp for the body. When your eyes are sound, your whole body is full of light; but when your eyes are no good, your whole body will be in darkness. Make certain, then, that the light in you is not darkness. If your whole body is full of light, with no part of it in darkness, it will be bright all over, as when a lamp shines on you with its brightness.

Jesus Accuses the Pharisees and the Teachers of the Law
Lk 11.39–44,46–52

To the Pharisee who was surprised that He had not washed before eating
Now then, you Pharisees clean the outside of your cup and plate, but inside you are full of violence and evil. Fools! Did not God, who made the outside, also make the inside? But give what is in your cups and plates to the poor, and everything will be ritually clean for you.

How terrible for you Pharisees! You give God a tenth of the seasoning herbs, such as mint and rue and all the other herbs, but you neglect justice and love for God. These you should practise, without neglecting the others.

How terrible for you Pharisees! You love the reserved seats in the synagogues and to be greeted with respect in the market-places. How terrible for you! You are like unmarked graves which people walk on without knowing it.

And to one of the teachers of the Law who said that Jesus was insulting them too when He said those things
How terrible also for you teachers of the Law! You put loads on people's backs which are hard to carry, but you yourselves will not stretch out a finger to help them carry those loads. How terrible for you! You make fine tombs for the prophets – the very prophets your ancestors murdered. You yourselves admit, then, that you approve of what your ancestors did; they murdered the prophets, and you build their tombs. For this reason the Wisdom of God said, 'I will send them prophets and messengers; they will kill some of them and persecute others.' So the people of this time will be punished for the murder of all the prophets killed since the creation of the world, from the murder of Abel to the murder of Zechariah, who was killed between the altar and the Holy Place. Yes, I tell you, the people of this time will be punished for them all!

How terrible for you teachers of the Law! You have kept the key that opens the door to the house of knowledge; you yourselves will not go in, and you stop those who are trying to go in!

A Warning against Hypocrisy
Lk 12.1–3

To His disciples as thousands of people crowded to hear Him
Be on guard against the yeast of the Pharisees – I mean their hypocrisy. Whatever is covered up will be uncovered, and every secret will be made known. So then, whatever you have said in the dark will be heard in broad daylight, and whatever you have

whispered in private in a closed room will be shouted from the housetops.

Whom to Fear
Lk 12.4–7

I tell you, my friends, do not be afraid of those who kill the body but cannot afterwards do anything worse. I will show you whom to fear: fear God, who, after killing, has the authority to throw into hell. Believe me, he is the one you must fear!

Aren't five sparrows sold for two pennies? Yet not one sparrow is forgotten by God. Even the hairs of your head have all been counted. So do not be afraid; you are worth much more than many sparrows!

Confessing and Rejecting Christ
Lk 12.8–12

I assure you that whoever declares publicly that he belongs to me, the Son of Man will do the same for him before the angels of God. But whoever rejects me publicly, the Son of Man will also reject him before the angels of God.

Anyone who says a word against the Son of Man can be forgiven; but whoever says evil things against the Holy Spirit will not be forgiven.

When they bring you to be tried in the synagogues or before governors or rulers, do not be worried about how you will defend yourself or what you will say. For the Holy Spirit will teach you at that time what you should say.

The Parable of the Rich Fool
Lk 12.14,15,16–21

When a man asked Him to sort out a family argument
My friend, who gave me the right to judge or to divide the property between you two?

To the crowd
Watch out and guard yourselves from every kind of greed; because a person's true life is not made up of the things he owns, no matter how rich he may be.

And as He told them a parable
There was once a rich man who had land which bore good crops. He began to think to himself, 'I haven't anywhere to keep all my crops. What can I do? This is what I will do,' he told himself; 'I will tear down my barns and build bigger ones, where I will store my corn and all my other goods. Then I will say to myself, Lucky man! You have all the good things you need for

many years. Take life easy, eat, drink, and enjoy yourself!' But God said to him, 'You fool! This very night you will have to give up your life; then who will get all these things you have kept for yourself?'

This is how it is with those who pile up riches for themselves but are not rich in God's sight.

Trust in God
Lk 12.22–31

Then to His disciples

And so I tell you not to worry about the food you need to stay alive or about the clothes you need for your body. Life is much more important than food, and the body much more important than clothes. Look at the crows: they don't sow seeds or gather a harvest; they don't have store-rooms or barns; God feeds them! You are worth so much more than birds! Can any of you live a bit longer by worrying about it? If you can't manage even such a small thing, why worry about the other things? Look how the wild flowers grow: they don't work or make clothes for themselves. But I tell you that not even King Solomon with all his wealth had clothes as beautiful as one of these flowers. It is God who clothes the wild grass – grass that is here today and gone tomorrow, burnt up in the oven. Won't he be all the more sure to clothe you? How little faith you have!

So don't be all upset, always concerned about what you will eat and drink. (For the pagans of this world are always concerned about all these things.) Your Father knows that you need these things. Instead, be concerned with his Kingdom, and he will provide you with these things.

Riches in Heaven
Lk 12.32–34

Do not be afraid, little flock, for your Father is pleased to give you the Kingdom. Sell all your belongings and give the money to the poor. Provide for yourselves purses that don't wear out, and save your riches in heaven, where they will never decrease, because no thief can get to them, and no moth can destroy them. For your heart will always be where your riches are.

Watchful Servants
Lk 12.35–40

Be ready for whatever comes, dressed for action and with your lamps lit, like servants who are waiting for their master to come back from a wedding feast. When he comes and knocks, they will open the door for him at once. How happy are those servants whose master finds them awake and ready when he returns! I tell you, he will take off his coat, ask them to sit down, and will wait on them. How happy they are if he finds them ready, even if he should come at midnight or even later! And you can be sure that if the owner of a house knew the time when the thief would come, he would not let the thief break into his house. And you, too, must be ready, because the Son of Man will come at an hour when you are not expecting him.

The Faithful or the Unfaithful Servant
Lk 12.42–48

When Peter asked whether this parable applied only to the disciples or to everyone

Who, then, is the faithful and wise servant? He is the one that his master will put in charge, to run the household and give the other servants their share of the food at the proper time. How happy that servant is if his master finds him doing this when he comes home! Indeed, I tell you, the master will put that servant in charge of all his property. But if that servant says to himself that his master is taking a long time to come back and if he begins to beat the other servants, both the men and the women, and eats and drinks and gets drunk, then the master will come back one day when the servant does not expect him and at a time he does not know. The master will cut him in pieces and make him share the fate of the disobedient.

The servant who knows what his master wants him to do, but does not get himself ready and do it, will be punished with a heavy whipping. But the servant who does not know what his master wants, and yet does something for which he deserves a whipping, will be punished with a light whipping. Much is required from the person to whom much is given; much more is required from the person to whom much more is given.

Jesus the Cause of Division
Lk 12.49–53

I came to set the earth on fire, and how I wish it were already kindled! I have a baptism to receive, and how distressed I am until it is over! Do you suppose that I came to bring peace to the world? No, not peace, but division. From now on a family of five will be divided, three against two and two against three. Fathers will be against their sons, and sons against their fathers; mothers will be against their daughters, and daughters against their mothers; mothers-in-law will be against their daughters-in-law, and daughters-in-law against their mothers-in-law.

Understanding the Time
Lk 12.54–56

And to the people

When you see a cloud coming up in the west, at once you say that it is going to rain – and it does. And when you feel the south wind blowing, you say that it is going to get hot – and it does. Hypocrites! You can look at the earth and the sky and predict the weather; why, then, don't you know the meaning of this present time?

Settle with Your Opponent
Lk 12.57–59

Why do you not judge for yourselves the right thing to do? If someone brings a lawsuit against you and takes you to court, do your best to settle the dispute with him before you get to court. If you don't, he will drag you before the judge, who will hand you over to the police, and you will be put in jail. There you will stay, I tell you, until you pay the last penny of your fine.

Turn from Your Sins or Die
Lk 13.2–5

To some people who told Him about the Galileans whom Pilate had killed
Because those Galileans were killed in that way, do you think it proves that they were worse sinners than all the other Galileans? No indeed! And I tell you that if you do not turn from your sins, you will all die as they did. What about those eighteen people in Siloam who were killed when the tower fell on them? Do you suppose this proves that they were worse than all the other people living in Jerusalem? No indeed! And I tell you that if you do not turn from your sins, you will all die as they did.

The Parable of the Unfruitful Fig-Tree
Lk 13.6–9

Then as He told them this parable
There was once a man who had a fig-tree growing in his vineyard. He went looking for figs on it but found none. So he said to his gardener, 'Look, for three years I have been coming here looking for figs on this fig-tree, and I haven't found any. Cut it down! Why should it go on using up the soil?' But the gardener answered, 'Leave it alone, sir, just one more year; I will dig round it and put in some manure. Then if the tree bears figs next year, so much the better; if not, then you can have it cut down.'

Jesus Heals a Crippled Woman on the Sabbath
Lk 13.12,15–16

In a synagogue one Sabbath, when He saw a woman who had been crippled by an evil spirit for many years
Woman, you are free from your illness!

And to an official of the synagogue who was angry that He had healed on the Sabbath
You hypocrites! Any one of you would untie his ox or his donkey from the stall and take it out to give it water on the Sabbath.

Now here is this descendant of Abraham whom Satan has kept bound up for eighteen years; should she not be released on the Sabbath?

The Parable of the Mustard Seed
Lk 13.18–19

What is the Kingdom of God like? What shall I compare it with? It is like this. A man takes a mustard seed and sows it in his field. The plant grows and becomes a tree, and the birds make their nests in its branches.

The Parable of the Yeast
Lk 13.20–21

What shall I compare the Kingdom of God with? It is like this. A woman takes some yeast and mixes it with forty litres of flour until the whole batch of dough rises.

The Narrow Door
Lk 13.24–30

When He was asked how many people would be saved
Do your best to go in through the narrow door; because many people will surely try to go in but will not be able. The master of the house will get up and close the door; then when you stand outside and begin to knock on the door and say, 'Open the door for us, sir!' he will answer you, 'I don't know where you come from!' Then you will answer, 'We ate and drank with you; you taught in our town!' But he will say again, 'I don't know where you come from. Get away from me, all you wicked people!' How you will cry and grind your teeth when you see Abraham, Isaac, and Jacob, and all the prophets in the Kingdom of God, while you are thrown out! People will come from the east and the west, from the north and the south, and sit down at the feast in the Kingdom of God. Then those who are now last will be first, and those who are now first will be last.

Jesus' Love for Jerusalem
Lk 13.32–35

When some Pharisees warned Him that He should leave because Herod wanted to kill Him
Go and tell that fox: 'I am driving out demons and performing cures today and tomorrow, and on the third day I shall finish my work.' Yet I must be on my way today, tomorrow, and the next day; it is not right for a prophet to be killed anywhere except in Jerusalem.

Jerusalem, Jerusalem! You kill the prophets, you stone the messengers God has sent you! How many times have I wanted to put my arms round all your people, just as a hen gathers her chicks under her wings, but you would not let me! And so your

Temple will be abandoned. I assure you that you will not see me until the time comes when you say, 'God bless him who comes in the name of the Lord.'

Jesus Heals a Sick Man
Lk 14.3,5

To some teachers of the Law and some Pharisees when a sick man came to Him on the Sabbath
Does our Law allow healing on the Sabbath or not?

When they would not answer, and He had healed the man and sent him away
If any one of you had a son or an ox that happened to fall in a well on a Sabbath, would you not pull him out at once on the Sabbath itself?

Humility and Hospitality
Lk 14.8–11,12–14

To some guests who were choosing the best places at a meal
When someone invites you to a wedding feast, do not sit down in the best place. It could happen that someone more important than you has been invited, and your host, who invited both of you, would have to come and say to you, 'Let him have this place.' Then you would be embarrassed and have to sit in the lowest place. Instead, when you are invited, go and sit in the lowest place, so that your host will come to you and say, 'Come on up, my friend, to a better place.' This will bring you honour in the presence of all the other guests. For everyone who makes himself great will be humbled, and everyone who humbles himself will be made great.

And to His host
When you give a lunch or a dinner, do not invite your friends or your brothers or your relatives or your rich neighbours – for they will invite you back, and in this way you will be paid for what you did. When you give a feast, invite the poor, the crippled, the lame, and the blind; and you will be blessed, because they are not able to pay you back. God will repay you on the day the good people rise from death.

The Parable of the Great Feast
Lk 14.16–24

To one of the men there, who said how happy those people would be who would sit at the feast in the Kingdom of God
There was once a man who was giving a great feast to which he invited many people. When it was time for the feast, he sent his servant to tell his guests, 'Come, everything is ready!' But they all began, one after another, to make excuses. The first one told the servant, 'I have bought a field and must go and look at it;

please accept my apologies.' Another one said, 'I have bought five pairs of oxen and am on my way to try them out; please accept my apologies.' Another one said, 'I have just got married, and for that reason I cannot come.'

The servant went back and told all this to his master. The master was furious and said to his servant, 'Hurry out to the streets and alleys of the town, and bring back the poor, the crippled, the blind, and the lame.' Soon the servant said, 'Your order has been carried out, sir, but there is room for more.' So the master said to the servant, 'Go out to the country roads and lanes and make people come in, so that my house will be full. I tell you all that none of those men who were invited will taste my dinner!'

The Cost of Being a Disciple
Lk 14.26–33

To some large crowds of people who were accompanying Him
Whoever comes to me cannot be my disciple unless he loves me more than he loves his father and his mother, his wife and his children, his brothers and his sisters, and himself as well. Whoever does not carry his own cross and come after me cannot be my disciple.

If one of you is planning to build a tower, he sits down first and works out what it will cost, to see if he has enough money to finish the job. If he doesn't, he will not be able to finish the tower after laying the foundations; and all who see what happened will laugh at him. 'This man began to build but can't finish the job!' they will say.

If a king goes out with ten thousand men to fight another king who comes against him with twenty thousand men, he will sit down first and decide if he is strong enough to face that other king. If he isn't he will send messengers to meet the other king, to ask for terms of peace while he is still a long way off. In the same way, none of you can be my disciple unless he gives up everything he has.

Worthless Salt
Lk 14.34–35

Salt is good, but if it loses its saltiness, there is no way to make it salty again. It is no good for the soil or for the manure heap; it is thrown away. Listen, then, if you have ears!

The Lost Sheep
Lk 15.4–7

To the Pharisees and teachers of the Law when tax collectors and other outcasts came to listen to Him

Suppose one of you has a hundred sheep and loses one of them – what does he do? He leaves the other ninety-nine sheep in the pasture and goes looking for the one that got lost until he finds it. When he finds it, he is so happy that he puts it on his shoulders and carries it back home. Then he calls his friends and neighbours together and says to them, 'I am so happy I found my lost sheep. Let us celebrate!' In the same way, I tell you, there will be more joy in heaven over one sinner who repents than over ninety-nine respectable people who do not need to repent.

The Lost Coin
Lk 15.8–10

Or suppose a woman who has ten silver coins loses one of them – what does she do? She lights a lamp, sweeps her house, and looks carefully everywhere until she finds it. When she finds it, she calls her friends and neighbours together, and says to them, 'I am so happy I found the coin I lost. Let us celebrate!' In the same way, I tell you, the angels of God rejoice over one sinner who repents.

The Lost Son
Lk 15.11–32

In another parable

There was once a man who had two sons. The younger one said to him, 'Father, give me my share of the property now.' So the man divided his property between his two sons. After a few days the younger son sold his part of the property and left home with the money. He went to a country far away, where he wasted his money in reckless living. He spent everything he had. Then a severe famine spread over that country, and he was left without a thing. So he went to work for one of the citizens of that country, who sent him out to his farm to take care of the pigs. He wished he could fill himself with the bean pods the pigs ate, but no one gave him anything to eat. At last he came to his senses and said, 'All my father's hired workers have more than they can eat, and here I am about to starve! I will get up and go to my father and say, Father, I have sinned against God and against you. I am no longer fit to be called your son; treat me as one of your hired workers.' So he got up and started back to his father.

He was still a long way from home when his father saw him; his heart was filled with pity, and he ran, threw his arms round his son, and kissed him. 'Father,' the son said, 'I have sinned against God and against you. I am no longer fit to be called your son.' But the father called his servants. 'Hurry!' he said. 'Bring the best robe and put it on him. Put a ring on his finger and shoes on his feet. Then go and get the prize calf and kill it, and let us celebrate with a feast! For this son of mine was dead, but now he is alive; he was lost, but now he has been found.' And so the feasting began.

In the meantime the elder son was out in the field. On his way back, when he came close to the house, he heard the music and dancing. So he called one of the servants and asked him, 'What's going on?' 'Your brother has come back home,' the servant answered, 'and your father has killed the prize calf, because he got him back safe and sound.'

The elder brother was so angry that he would not go into the house; so his father came out and begged him to come in. But he answered his father, 'Look, all these years I have worked for you like a slave, and I have never disobeyed your orders. What have you given me? Not even a goat for me to have a feast with my friends! But this son of yours wasted all your property on prostitutes, and when he comes back home, you kill the prize calf for him!' 'My son,' the father answered, 'you are always here with me, and everything I have is yours. But we had to celebrate and be happy, because your brother was dead, but now he is alive; he was lost, but now he has been found.'

The Shrewd Manager
Lk 16.1–13

To His disciples
There was once a rich man who had a servant who managed his property. The rich man was told that the manager was wasting his master's money, so he called him in and said, 'What is this I hear about you? Hand in a complete account of your handling of my property, because you cannot be my manager any longer.' The servant said to himself, 'My Master is going to dismiss me from my job. What shall I do? I am not strong enough to dig ditches, and I am ashamed to beg. Now I know what I will do! Then when my job is gone, I shall have friends who will welcome me in their homes.'

So he called in all the people who were in debt to his master. He asked the first one, 'How much do you owe my master?' 'One hundred barrels of olive-oil,' he answered. 'Here is your account,' the manager told him; 'sit down and write fifty.' Then he asked another one, 'And you – how much do you owe?' 'A thousand sacks of wheat,' he answered. 'Here is your account,' the manager told him; 'write eight hundred.'

As a result the master of this dishonest manager praised him for doing such a shrewd thing; because the people of this world are much more shrewd in handling their affairs than the people who belong to the light.

And so I tell you; make friends for yourselves with worldly wealth, so that when it gives out, you will be welcomed in the eternal home. Whoever is faithful in small matters will be faithful in large ones; whoever is dishonest in small matters will be dishonest in large ones. If then, you have not been faithful in handling worldly wealth, how can you be trusted with true wealth? And if you have not been faithful with what belongs to someone else, who will give you what belongs to you?

No servant can be the slave of two masters; he will hate one and love the other; he will be loyal to one and despise the other. You cannot serve both God and money.

Some Sayings of Jesus
Lk 16.15–18

To the Pharisees who sneered at Jesus' teaching because they loved money
You are the ones who make yourselves look right in other people's sight, but God knows your hearts. For the things that are considered of great value by man are worth nothing in God's sight.

The Law of Moses and the writings of the prophets were in effect up to the time of John the Baptist; since then the Good News about the Kingdom of God is being told, and everyone forces his way in. But it is easier for heaven and earth to disappear than for the smallest detail of the Law to be done away with.

Any man who divorces his wife and marries another woman commits adultery; and the man who marries a divorced woman commits adultery.

The Rich Man and Lazarus
Lk 16.19–31

There was once a rich man who dressed in the most expensive clothes and lived in great luxury every day. There was also a poor man named Lazarus, covered with sores, who used to be brought to the rich man's door, hoping to eat the bits of food that fell from the rich man's table. Even the dogs would come and lick his sores.

The poor man died and was carried by the angels to sit beside Abraham at the feast in heaven. The rich man died and was buried, and in Hades, where he was in great pain, he looked up and saw Abraham, far away, with Lazarus at his side. So he called out, 'Father Abraham! Take pity on me, and send Lazarus to dip his finger in some water and cool my tongue, because I am in great pain in this fire!'

But Abraham said, 'Remember, my son, that in your lifetime you were given all the good things, while Lazarus got all the bad things. But now he is enjoying himself here, while you are in pain. Besides all that, there is a deep pit lying between us, so that those who want to cross over from here to you cannot do so, nor can anyone cross over to us from where you are.' The rich man said, 'Then I beg you, father Abraham, send Lazarus to my father's house, where I have five brothers. Let him go and warn them so that they, at least, will not come to this place of pain.'

Abraham said, 'Your brothers have Moses and the prophets to warn them; your brothers should listen to what they say.' The rich man answered, 'That is not enough, father Abraham! But if someone were to rise from death and go to them, then they would turn from their sins.' But Abraham said, 'If they will not listen to Moses and the prophets, they will not be convinced even if someone were to rise from death.'

Sin
Lk 17.1–4

To His disciples

Things that make people fall into sin are bound to happen, but how terrible for the one who makes them happen! It would be better for him if a large millstone were tied round his neck and he were thrown into the sea than for him to cause one of these little ones to sin. So watch what you do!

If your brother sins, rebuke him, and if he repents, forgive him. If he sins against you seven times in one day, and each time he comes to you saying, 'I repent,' you must forgive him.

Faith
Lk 17.6

To the apostles who asked the Lord to increase their faith

If you had faith as big as a mustard seed, you could say to this mulberry tree, 'Pull yourself up by the roots and plant yourself in the sea!' and it would obey you.

A Servant's Duty
Lk 17.7–10

Suppose one of you has a servant who is ploughing or looking after the sheep. When he comes in from the field, do you tell him to hurry and eat his meal? Of course not! Instead, you say to him, 'Get my supper ready, then put on your apron and wait on me while I eat and drink; after that you may have your meal.' The servant does not deserve thanks for obeying orders, does he? It is the same with you; when you have done all you have been told to do, say, 'We are ordinary servants; we have only done our duty.'

Jesus Heals Ten Men
Lk 17.14,17–18,19

To ten men suffering from a dreaded skin-disease who implored Him to help them
Go and let the priests examine you.

When one of the men, a Samaritan, returned to thank Him for healing him.
There were ten men who were healed; where are the other nine? Why is this foreigner the only one who came back to give thanks to God?

And to the man who had returned
Get up and go; your faith has made you well.

The Coming of the Kingdom
Lk 17.20–21,22–35,37

To some Pharisees who asked Jesus when the Kingdom of God would come
The Kingdom of God does not come in such a way as to be seen. No one will say, 'Look, here it is!'; or, 'There it is!'; because the Kingdom of God is within you.

Then to His disciples
The time will come when you will wish you could see one of the days of the Son of Man, but you will not see it. There will be those who will say to you, 'Look, over there!' or, 'Look, over here!' But don't go out looking for it. As the lightning flashes across the sky and lights it up from one side to the other, so will the Son of Man be in his day. But first he must suffer much and be rejected by the people of this day. As it was in the time of Noah so shall it be in the days of the Son of Man. Everybody kept on eating and drinking, and men and women married, up to the very day Noah went into the boat and the flood came and killed them all. It will be as it was in the time of Lot. Everybody

kept on eating and drinking, buying and selling, planting and building. On the day Lot left Sodom, fire and sulphur rained down from heaven and killed them all. That is how it will be on the day the Son of Man is revealed.

On that day the man who is on the roof of his house must not go down into the house to get his belongings; in the same way the man who is out in the field must not go back to the house. Remember Lot's wife! Whoever tries to save his own life will lose it; whoever loses his life will save it. On that night, I tell you, there will be two people sleeping in the same bed: one will be taken away, the other will be left behind. Two women will be grinding corn together: one will be taken away, the other will be left behind.

And when His disciples asked Him where these things would happen
Wherever there is a dead body the vultures will gather.

The Parable
of the Widow and the Judge
Lk 18.2–8

To His disciples when He taught them always to pray and never become discouraged
In a certain town there was a judge who neither feared God nor respected man. And there was a widow in that same town who kept coming to him and pleading for her rights, saying, 'Help me against my opponent!' For a long time the judge refused to act, but at last he said to himself, 'Even though I don't fear God or respect man, yet because of all the trouble this widow is giving me, I will see to it that she gets her rights. If I don't, she will keep on coming and finally wear me out!'

And as He continued
Listen to what that corrupt judge said. Now, will God not judge in favour of his own people who cry to him day and night for help? Will he be slow to help them? I tell you, he will judge in their favour and do it quickly. But will the Son of Man find faith on earth when he comes?

The Parable
of the Pharisee
and the Tax Collector
Lk 18.10–14

In a parable to people who were sure of their own goodness and despised everybody else
Once there were two men who went up to the Temple to pray: one was a Pharisee, the other a tax collector.

The Pharisee stood apart by himself and prayed, 'I thank you, God, that I am not greedy, dishonest, or an adulterer, like everybody else. I thank you that I am not like that tax collector over there. I fast two days a week, and I give you a tenth of all my income.

But the tax collector stood at a distance and would not even raise his face to heaven, but beat on his breast and said, 'God, have pity on me, a sinner!' I tell you, the tax collector, and not the Pharisee, was in the right with God when he went home. For everyone who makes himself great will be humbled, and everyone who humbles himself will be made great.

Jesus Blesses Little Children
Lk 18.16–17

To His disciples when they tried to stop people bringing their children to Him
Let the children come to me and do not stop them, because the Kingdom of God belongs to such as these. Remember this! Whoever does not receive the Kingdom of God like a child will never enter it.

The Rich Man
Lk 18.19–20,22,24–25,27,29–30

To the Jewish leader who asked Him what he should do to receive eternal life
Why do you call me good? No one is good except God alone. You know the commandments: 'Do not commit adultery; do not commit murder; do not steal; do not accuse anyone falsely; respect your father and your mother.'

When the man said he had obeyed all these commandments since he was young
There is still one more thing you need to do. Sell all you have and give the money to the poor, and you will have riches in heaven; then come and follow me.

When the man became sad at hearing this because he was rich
How hard it is for rich people to enter the Kingdom of God! It is much harder for a rich person to enter the Kingdom of God than for a camel to go through the eye of a needle.

When the people asked Him who could be saved
What is impossible for man is possible for God.

And when Peter said that he and others had left their homes to follow Him
Yes, and I assure you that anyone who leaves home or wife or brothers or parents or children for the sake of the Kingdom of

God will receive much more in this present age and eternal life in the age to come.

Jesus Speaks a Third Time about His Death
Lk 18.31–33

To His disciples concerning His death
Listen! We are going to Jerusalem where everything the prophets wrote about the Son of Man will come true. He will be handed over to the Gentiles, who will mock him, insult him, and spit on him. They will whip him and kill him, but three days later he will rise to life.

Jesus Heals a Blind Beggar
Lk 18.41,42

When a blind man asked for His help
What do you want me to do for you?

When the man said he wanted to see again
Then see! Your faith has made you well.

Jesus and Zacchaeus
Lk 19.5,9–10

To Zacchaeus, a chief tax collector in Jericho, who had climbed a tree to see Him pass by
Hurry down, Zacchaeus, because I must stay in your house today.

When Zacchaeus promised to give half his belongings to the poor, and more than repay those whom he had cheated
Salvation has come to this house today, for this man, also, is a descendant of Abraham. The Son of Man came to seek and to save the lost.

The Parable of the Gold Coins
Lk 19.12–27

To the people who supposed, now that they were near Jerusalem, that the Kingdom of God was about to appear
There was once a man of high rank who was going to a country far away to be made king, after which he planned to come back home. Before he left, he called his ten servants and gave them each a gold coin and told them, 'See what you can earn with this while I am gone.' Now, his countrymen hated him, and so they sent messengers after him to say, 'We don't want this man to be our king.'

The man was made king and came back. At once he ordered his servants to appear before him, in order to find out how much they had earned. The first one came and said, 'Sir, I have earned ten gold coins with the one you gave me.' 'Well done,' he said; 'you are a good servant! Since you were faithful in small matters, I will put you in charge of ten cities.' The second servant came and said, 'Sir, I have earned five gold coins with the one you gave me.' To this one he said, 'You will be in charge of five cities.'

Another servant came and said, 'Sir, here is your gold coin; I kept it hidden in a handkerchief. I was afraid of you, because you are a hard man. You take what is not yours and reap what you did not sow.' He said to him, 'You bad servant! I will use your own words to condemn you! You know that I am a hard man, taking what is not mine and reaping what I have not sown. Well, then, why didn't you put my money in the bank? Then I would have received it back with interest when I returned.'

Then he said to those who were standing there, 'Take the gold coin away from him and give it to the servant who has ten coins.' But they said to him, 'Sir, he already has ten coins!' 'I tell you,' he replied, 'that to every person who has something, even more will be given; but the person who has nothing, even the little that he has will be taken away from him. Now, as for those enemies of mine who did not want me to be their king, bring them here and kill them in my presence!'

The Triumphant Approach to Jerusalem
Lk 19.30–31,40

To two of His disciples as they approached Jerusalem
Go to the village there ahead of you; as you go in, you will find a colt tied up that has never been ridden. Untie it and bring it here. If someone asks you why you are untying it, tell him that the Master needs it.

When the Pharisees asked Him to quieten the large crowd of disciples who were cheering Him and calling Him their king
I tell you that if they keep quiet, the stones themselves will start shouting.

Jesus Weeps over Jerusalem
Lk 19.42–44

As He came closer to the city and wept over it
If you only knew today what is needed for peace! But now you cannot see it! The time will come when your enemies will surround you with barricades, blockade you, and close in on you from every side. They will completely destroy you and the people within your walls; not a single stone will they leave in its place, because you did not recognize the time when God came to save you!

Jesus Goes to the Temple
Lk 19.46

When He drove the merchants out of the Temple
It is written in the Scriptures that God said, 'My Temple will be

called a house of prayer.' But you have turned it into a hideout for thieves!

The Question about Jesus' Authority
Lk 20.3–4,8

To the chief priests, teachers of the Law, and elders in the Temple when they questioned His authority
Now let me ask you a question. Tell me, did John's right to baptize come from God or from man?

And when they would not answer for fear of what the people might do
Neither will I tell you, then, by what right I do these things.

The Parable of the Tenants in the Vineyard
Lk 20.9–16,17–18

As He told the people this parable
There was once a man who planted a vineyard, let it out to tenants, and then left home for a long time. When the time came to gather the grapes, he sent a slave to the tenants to receive from them his share of the harvest. But the tenants beat the slave and sent him back without a thing. So he sent another slave; but the tenants beat him also, treated him shamefully, and sent him back without a thing. Then he sent a third slave; the tenants wounded him, too, and threw him out. Then the owner of the vineyard said, 'What shall I do? I will send my own dear son; surely they will respect him!' But when the tenants saw him, they said to one another, 'This is the owner's son. Let's kill him, and his property will be ours!' So they threw him out of the vineyard and killed him.

What, then, will the owner of the vineyard do to the tenants? He will come and kill those men, and hand the vineyard over to other tenants.

When the people expressed disbelief
What, then, does this scripture mean?
'The stone which the builders rejected as worthless
   turned out to be the most important of all.'
Everyone who falls on that stone will be cut to pieces; and if that stone falls on someone, it will crush him to dust.

The Question about Paying Taxes
Lk 20.24,25

In answer to a trick question asked by some spies sent by the Pharisees
Show me a silver coin. Whose face and name are these on it?

When they said they were the Emperor's
Well, then, pay the Emperor what belongs to the Emperor, and pay God what belongs to God.

The Question about Rising from Death	*When the Sadducees, who did not believe that people rise from the dead, asked Him about it*

The Question about Rising from Death
Lk 20.34–38

When the Sadducees, who did not believe that people rise from the dead, asked Him about it

The men and women of this age marry, but the men and women who are worthy to rise from death and live in the age to come will not then marry. They will be like angels and cannot die. They are the sons of God, because they have risen from death. And Moses clearly proves that the dead are raised to life. In the passage about the burning bush he speaks of the Lord as 'the God of Abraham, the God of Isaac, and the God of Jacob.' He is the God of the living, not of the dead, for to him all are alive.

The Question about the Messiah
Lk 20.41–44

To the teachers of the Law

How can it be said that the Messiah will be the descendant of David? For David himself says in the books of Psalms,
The Lord said to my Lord:
    Sit here on my right
until I put your enemies as a footstool under your feet.'
David called him 'Lord'; how, then, can the Messiah be David's descendant?

Jesus Warns against the Teachers of the Law
Lk 20.46–47

To His disciples as the people listened to Him

Be on your guard against the teachers of the Law, who like to walk about in their long robes and love to be greeted with respect in the market-place; who choose the reserved seats in the synagogues and the best places at feasts; who take advantage of widows and rob them of their homes, and then make a show of saying long prayers! Their punishment will be all the worse!

The Widow's Offering
Lk 21.3–4

When He saw a very poor widow dropping two small coins in the temple treasury

I tell you that this poor widow put in more than all the others. For the others offered their gifts from what they had to spare of their riches; but she, poor as she is, gave all she had to live on.

Jesus Speaks of the Destruction of the Temple
Lk 21.6

As His disciples were discussing the beauty of the Temple

All this you see – the time will come when not a single stone here will be left in its place; every one will be thrown down.

Troubles and Persecutions
Lk 21.8–19

When the disciples asked when this would happen and how they would know that the time had come

Be on guard; don't be deceived. Many men, claiming to speak for me, will come and say, 'I am he!' and, 'The time has come!' But don't follow them. Don't be afraid when you hear of wars and revolutions; such things must happen first, but they do not mean that the end is near.

Countries will fight each other; kingdoms will attack one another. There will be terrible earthquakes, famines, and plagues everywhere; there will be strange and terrifying things coming from the sky. Before all these things take place, however, you will be arrested and persecuted; and you will be handed over to be tried in synagogues and be put in prison; you will be brought before kings and rulers for my sake. This will be your chance to tell the Good News. Make up your minds beforehand not to worry about how you will defend yourselves, because I will give you such words and wisdom that none of your enemies will be able to refute or contradict what you say. You will be handed over by your parents, your brothers, your relatives, and your friends; and some of you will be put to death. Everyone will hate you because of me. But not a single hair from your heads will be lost. Stand firm, and you will save yourselves.

Jesus Speaks of the Destruction of Jerusalem
Lk 21.20–24

When you see Jerusalem surrounded by armies, then you will know that she will soon be destroyed. Then those who are in Judaea must run away to the hills; those who are in the city must leave, and those who are out in the country must not go into the city. For those will be 'The Days of Punishment,' to make all that the Scriptures say come true. How terrible it will be in those days for women who are pregnant and for mothers with little babies! Terrible distress will come upon this land, and God's punishment will fall on this people. Some will be killed by the sword, and others will be taken as prisoners to all countries; and the heathen will trample over Jerusalem until their time is up.

The Coming of the Son of Man
Lk 21.25–28

There will be strange things happening to the sun, the moon, and the stars. On earth whole countries will be in despair, afraid of the roar of the sea and the raging tides. People will faint from fear as they wait for what is coming over the whole earth, for the powers in space will be driven from their courses. Then the Son of Man will appear, coming in a cloud with great power and glory. When these things begin to happen, stand up and raise your heads, because your salvation is near.

The Lesson of the Fig-Tree
Lk 21.29–33

As He told them this parable
Think of the fig-tree and all the other trees. When you see their

leaves beginning to appear, you know that summer is near. In the same way, when you see things happening, you will know that the Kingdom of God is about to come.

Remember that all these things will take place before the people now living have all died. Heaven and earth will pass away, but my words will never pass away.

The Need to Watch
Lk 21.34–36

Be on your guard! Don't let yourselves become occupied with too much feasting and drinking and with the worries of this life, or that Day may suddenly catch you like a trap. For it will come upon all people everywhere on earth. Be on the alert and pray always that you will have the strength to go safely through all those things that will happen and to stand before the Son of Man.

Jesus Prepares to Eat the Passover Meal
Lk 22.8,10–12

To Peter and John
Go and get the Passover meal ready for us to eat.

When they asked Him where He wanted it prepared
As you go into the city, a man carrying a jar of water will meet you. Follow him into the house that he enters, and say to the owner of the house: 'The Teacher says to you, Where is the room where my disciples and I will eat the Passover meal?' He will show you a large furnished room upstairs, where you will get everything ready.

The Lord's Supper
Lk 22.15,17–18,19,20,21–22

When He took His place at the table with the apostles
I have wanted so much to eat this Passover meal with you before I suffer! For I tell you, I will never eat it until it is given its full meaning in the Kingdom of God.

As He took a cup and gave thanks to God
Take this and share it among yourselves. I tell you that from now on I will not drink this wine until the Kingdom of God comes.

And as He took a piece of bread, gave thanks to God, broke it, and gave it to them
This is my body, which is given for you. Do this in memory of me.

After supper, as He handed them the cup
This cup is God's new covenant sealed with my blood, which is poured out for you.

About the man who would betray Him
But, look! The one who betrays me is here at the table with me! The Son of Man will die as God has decided, but how terrible for that man who betrays him!

The Argument about Greatness
Lk 22.25–30

To His disciples when they argued over which one of them should be thought of as the greatest
The kings of the pagans have power over their people, and the rulers are called 'Friends of the People.' But this is not the way it is with you; rather, the greatest one among you must be like the youngest, and the leader must be like the servant. Who is greater, the one who sits down to eat or the one who serves him? The one who sits down, of course. But I am among you as one who serves.

You have stayed with me all through my trials; and just as my Father has given me the right to rule, so I will give you the same right. You will eat and drink at my table in my Kingdom, and you will sit on thrones to rule over the twelve tribes of Israel.

Jesus Predicts Peter's Denial
Lk 22.31–32,34

To Peter
Simon, Simon! Listen! Satan has received permission to test all of you, to separate the good from the bad, as a farmer separates the wheat from the chaff. But I have prayed for you, Simon, that your faith will not fail. And when you turn back to me, you must strengthen your brothers.

And when Peter said that he was ready to go to prison with Him and to die with Him
I tell you, Peter, the cock will not crow tonight until you have said three times that you do not know me.

Purse, Bag and Sword
Lk 22.35,36–37,38

To His disciples
When I sent you out that time without purse, bag, or shoes, did you lack anything?

When they said that they had not
But now, whoever has a purse or a bag must take it; and whoever has no sword must sell his coat and buy one. For I tell

you that the scripture which says, 'He shared the fate of criminals,' must come true about me, because what was written about me is coming true.

And when they showed Him they had two swords
That is enough.

Jesus Prays on the Mount of Olives
Lk 22.40,42,46

To His disciples when they had gone with Him to the Mount of Olives
Pray that you will not fall into temptation.

Then as He went a short distance away from them, and knelt down and prayed
Father, if you will, take this cup of suffering away from me. Not my will, however, but your will be done.

After He had returned to His disciples and found them asleep
Why are you sleeping? Get up and pray that you will not fall into temptation.

The Arrest of Jesus
Lk 22.48,51,52–53

When Judas, at the head of a crowd, came up to Jesus and kissed Him
Judas, is it with a kiss that you betray the Son of Man?

And when one of His disciples struck the High Priest's slave and cut off his right ear
Enough of this!

To the chief priests, the officers of the temple guard, and the elders who had come there to get Him
Did you have to come with swords and clubs, as though I were an outlaw? I was with you in the Temple every day, and you did not try to arrest me. But this is your hour to act, when the power of darkness rules.

Peter Denies Jesus
Lk 22.61

As recalled by Peter
Before the cock crows tonight, you will say three times that you do not know me.

Jesus Is Brought before the Council
Lk 22.67–69,70

When He was brought before the Council and they asked Him if He was the Messiah
If I tell you, you will not believe me; and if I ask you a question, you will not answer. But from now on the Son of Man will be seated on the right of Almighty God.

And when they asked Him if then He was the Son of God
You say that I am.

Jesus Is Brought
before Pilate
Lk 23.3

When He was brought before Pilate who asked Him if He was the King of the Jews
So you say.

Jesus Is Crucified
Lk 23.28–31,34,42

To some women who were weeping for Him as He was being led away to be crucified
Women of Jerusalem! Don't cry for me, but for yourselves and your children. For the days are coming when people will say, 'How lucky are the women who never had children, who never bore babies, who never nursed them!' That will be the time when people will say to the mountains, 'Fall on us!' and to the hills, 'Hide us!' For if such things as these are done when the wood is green, what will happen when it is dry?

As they crucified Him along with two criminals
Forgive them, Father! They don't know what they are doing.

When one of the criminals asked Him to remember him
I promise you that today you will be in Paradise with me.

The Death of Jesus
Lk 23.46

From the cross, just before He died
Father! In your hands I place my spirit!

The Walk to Emmaus
Lk 24.17,19,25–26

After His resurrection, when He met Cleopas and another disciple, neither of whom recognized Him
What are you talking about to each other, as you walk along?

When they asked Him whether He had not heard of the things that had been happening in Jerusalem during those past few days
What things?

When they told Him about the crucifixion, the empty tomb and the news of the resurrection
How foolish you are, how slow you are to believe everything the prophets said! Was it not necessary for the Messiah to suffer these things and then to enter his glory?

Jesus Appears
to His Disciples
Lk 24.36,38–39,41,44,46–49

After Cleopas and his companion had returned to the eleven disciples in Jerusalem, and Jesus Himself suddenly stood among them
Peace be with you.

When they were terrified, thinking they were seeing a ghost
Why are you alarmed? Why are these doubts coming up in your minds? Look at my hands and my feet, and see that it is I myself. Feel me, and you will know, for a ghost doesn't have flesh and bones, as you can see I have.

And when He had shown them His hands and feet, and still they could not believe
Have you anything here to eat?

To show them that His teaching had been leading to these events
These are the very things I told you about while I was still with you: everything written about me in the Law of Moses, the writings of the prophets, and the Psalms had to come true.

To help His disciples understand the Scriptures
This is what is written: the Messiah must suffer and must rise from death three days later, and in his name the message about repentance and the forgiveness of sins must be preached to all nations, beginning in Jerusalem. You are witnesses of these things. And I myself will send upon you what my Father has promised. But you must wait in the city until the power from above comes down upon you.

Christ's
Words

in John

Christ's Words in John

The First Disciples of Jesus
Jn 1.38,39,42

To two men who followed Him, after their teacher John the Baptist had declared Him to be the Lamb of God
What are you looking for?

When they asked Him where He lived
Come and see.

When Simon Peter came to Him after hearing He was the Messiah
Your name is Simon, son of John, but you will be called Cephas.

Jesus Calls Philip and Nathanael
Jn 1.43,47,48,50–51

To Philip when He decided to go to Galilee
Come with me!

When Philip had brought Nathanael to Jesus
Here is a real Israelite; there is nothing false in him!

When Nathanael asked how He knew him
I saw you when you were under the fig-tree before Philip called you.

And when Nathanael then exclaimed that Jesus was the Son of God, the King of Israel
Do you believe just because I told you I saw you when you were under the fig-tree? You will see much greater things than this! I am telling you the truth: you will see heaven open and God's angels going up and coming down on the Son of Man.

The Wedding in Cana
Jn 2.4,7,8,

To His mother at a wedding, when she told Him they had no wine left
You must not tell me what to do. My time has not yet come.

Then to the servants
Fill these jars with water.

And when they had filled them to the brim
Now draw some water out and take it to the man in charge of the feast.

Jesus Goes to the Temple
Jn 2.16,19

When He cleared the Temple of the money-changers and the men who sold animals and birds
Take them out of here! Stop making my Father's house a market-place!

And when the Jewish authorities asked what miracle He could perform to show them He had the right to do this
Tear down this Temple, and in three days I will build it again.

Jesus and Nicodemus
Jn 3.3,5–8,10–13

To Nicodemus, a Jewish leader, who recognized that He was a teacher sent by God, and came to see Him at night
I am telling you the truth: no one can see the Kingdom of God unless he is born again.

When Nicodemus asked how a grown man could be born again
I am telling you the truth. No one can enter the Kingdom of God unless he is born of water and the Spirit. A person is born physically of human parents, but he is born spiritually of the Spirit. Do not be surprised because I tell you that you must all be born again. The wind blows wherever it wishes; you hear the sound it makes, but you do not know where it comes from or where it is going. It is like that with everyone who is born of the Spirit.

And when he asked again how this could be
You are a great teacher in Israel, and you don't know this? I am telling you the truth: we speak of what we know and report what we have seen, yet none of you is willing to accept our message. You do not believe me when I tell you about the things of this world; how will you ever believe me, then, when I tell you about the things of heaven? And no one has ever gone up to heaven except the Son of Man, who came down from heaven.

Jesus and the Samaritan Woman
Jn 4.7,10,13–14,16,17–18, 21–24,26,32,34–38

To the Samaritan woman whom He met at Jacob's Well
Give me a drink of water.

When the woman asked how He, a Jew, could ask her, a Samaritan, for a drink
If only you knew what God gives and who it is that is asking you for a drink, you would ask him, and he would give you life-giving water.

When the woman asked how He would obtain that life-giving water
Whoever drinks this water will be thirsty again, but whoever
drinks the water that I will give him will never be thirsty again.
The water that I will give him will become in him a spring
which will provide him with life-giving water and give him
eternal life.

*When the woman asked to be given that water, that she might never be
thirsty again nor have to come again to the well*
Go and call your husband, and come back.

When she said she did not have a husband
You are right when you say you haven't got a husband. You
have been married to five men, and the man you live with now
is not really your husband. You have told me the truth.

*When she then said that He was a prophet, and remarked that the
Samaritans worshipped God on the mountain, whereas the Jews
worshipped Him in Jerusalem.*
Believe me, woman, the time will come when people will not
worship the Father either on this mountain or in Jerusalem. You
Samaritans do not really know whom you worship; but we Jews
know whom we worship, because it is from the Jews that
salvation comes. But the time is coming and is already here,
when by the power of God's Spirit people will worship the
Father as he really is, offering him the true worship that he
wants. God is Spirit, and only by the power of his Spirit can
people worship him as he really is.

*And when the woman said that she knew that the Messiah would come and
tell them everything*
I am he, I who am talking with you.

*To His disciples, after the woman had left, when they implored Him to
eat something*
I have food to eat that you know nothing about.

*And when the disciples then started asking among themselves whether
somebody could have brought Him some food*
My food is to obey the will of the one who sent me and to finish
the work he gave me to do. You have a saying, 'Four more
months and then the harvest.' But I tell you, take a good look at
the fields; the crops are now ripe and ready to be harvested! The

man who reaps the harvest is being paid and gathers the crops for eternal life; so the man who sows and the man who reaps will be glad together. The saying is true, 'One man sows, another man reaps.' I have sent you to reap a harvest in a field where you did not work; others worked there, and you profit from their work.

Jesus Heals an Official's Son
Jn 4.48,50,53

Back in Cana, in Galilee, when a government official asked Jesus to go to Capernaum to heal his son
None of you will ever believe unless you see miracles and wonders.

And when the official begged Him to come before the boy died
Go, your son will live!

As recalled by the official
Your son will live.

The Healing at the Pool
Jn 5.6,8,14,17

By the pool in Jerusalem, to a man who had been ill for thirty-eight years
Do you want to get well?

When the man said that he could not get into the pool in time
Get up, pick up your mat, and walk.

Later, when Jesus found the man in the Temple after he had been unable to tell the Jewish authorities who it was who had healed him on the Sabbath
Listen, you are well now; so stop sinning or something worse may happen to you.

To the Jewish authorities because they began to persecute Him for healing the man on the Sabbath Day
My Father is always working, and I too must work.

The Authority of the Son
Jn 5.19–29

To the Jewish authorities who were then determined to kill Him, not only for having broken the Sabbath law, but also for making Himself equal with God, by saying that God was His Father
I am telling you the truth: the Son can do nothing on his own; he does only what he sees his Father doing. What the Father does, the Son also does. For the Father loves the Son and shows him all that he himself is doing. He will show him even greater things to do than this, and you will all be amazed. Just as the Father raises the dead and gives them life, in the same way the

Son gives life to those he wants to. Nor does the Father himself judge anyone. He has given his Son the full right to judge, so that all will honour the Son in the same way as they honour the Father. Whoever does not honour the Son does not honour the Father who sent him.

I am telling you the truth: whoever hears my words and believes in him who sent me has eternal life. He will not be judged, but has already passed from death to life. I am telling you the truth: the time is coming – the time has already come – when the dead will hear the voice of the Son of God, and those who hear it will come to life. Just as the Father is himself the source of life, in the same way he has made his Son to be the source of life. And he has given the Son the right to judge, because he is the Son of Man. Do not be surprised at this; the time is coming when all the dead will hear his voice and come out of their graves: those who have done good will rise and live, and those who have done evil will rise and be condemned.

Witnesses to Jesus
Jn 5.30–47

I can do nothing on my own authority; I judge only as God tells me, so my judgement is right, because I am not trying to do what I want, but only what he who sent me wants.

If I testify on my own behalf, what I say is not to be accepted as real proof. But there is someone else who testifies on my behalf, and I know that what he says about me is true. John is the one to whom you sent your messengers, and he spoke on behalf of the truth. It is not that I must have a man's witness; I say this only in order that you may be saved. John was like a lamp, burning and shining, and you were willing for a while to enjoy his light. But I have a witness on my behalf which is even greater than the witness that John gave: what I do, that is, the deeds my Father gave me to do, these speak on my behalf and show that the Father has sent me. And the Father, who sent me, also testifies on my behalf. You have never heard his voice or seen his face, and you do not keep his message in your hearts, for you do not believe in the one whom he sent. You study the Scriptures, because you think that in them you will find eternal life. And these very Scriptures speak about me! Yet you are not willing to come to me in order to have life.

I am not looking for human praise. But I know what kind of people you are, and I know that you have no love for God in your hearts. I have come with my Father's authority, but you have not received me; when, however, someone comes with his own authority, you will receive him. You like to receive praise from one another, but you do not try to win praise from the one who alone is God; how then can you believe me? Do not think, however, that I am the one who will accuse you to my Father. Moses, in whom you have put your hope, is the very one who will accuse you. If you had really believed Moses, you would have believed me, because he wrote about me. But since you do not believe what he wrote, how can you believe what I say?

Jesus Feeds Five Thousand Men
Jn 6.5,10,12

To Philip, when a large crowd had followed Him
Where can we buy enough food to feed all these people?

When Andrew said there was a boy there with five loaves of barley bread and two fish only
Make the people sit down.

When He had taken the bread and the fish, given thanks to God and distributed them, and everyone had eaten as much as they wanted
Gather the pieces left over; let us not waste any.

Jesus Walks on the Water
Jn 6.20

When the disciples were in a boat on their way back across the lake towards Capernaum, and they saw Jesus walking towards them on the water
Don't be afraid, it is I!

Jesus the Bread of Life
Jn 6.26–27,29,32–33,35–40, 43–51,53–58

To the people when they found Jesus back on the other side of the lake, and asked Him when He got there
I am telling you the truth: you are looking for me because you ate the bread and had all you wanted, not because you understood my miracles. Do not work for food that goes bad; instead, work for the food that lasts for eternal life. This is the food which the Son of Man will give you, because God, the Father, has put his mark of approval on him.

When they asked Him how they could do God's will
What God wants you to do is to believe in the one he sent.

And when they asked Him if He would perform a miracle so that they might believe Him, just as Moses had given their ancestors manna in the desert
I am telling you the truth. What Moses gave you was not the

bread from heaven; it is my Father who gives you the real bread from heaven. For the bread that God gives is he who comes down from heaven and gives life to the world.

And when they asked to be given that bread
I am the bread of life. He who comes to me will never be hungry; he who believes in me will never be thirsty. Now, I told you that you have seen me but will not believe. Everyone whom my Father gives me will come to me. I will never turn away anyone who comes to me, because I have come down from heaven to do not my own will but the will of him who sent me. And it is the will of him who sent me that I should not lose any of all those he has given me, but that I should raise them all to life on the last day. For what my Father wants is that all who see the Son and believe in him should have eternal life. And I will raise them to life on the last day.

When the people started grumbling at Jesus' words, saying He was only the son of Joseph
Stop grumbling among yourselves. No one can come to me unless the Father who sent me draws him to me; and I will raise him to life on the last day. The prophets wrote, 'Everyone will be taught by God.' Anyone who hears the Father and learns from him comes to me. This does not mean that anyone has seen the Father; he who is from God is the only one who has seen the Father. I am telling you the truth: he who believes has eternal life. I am the bread of life. Your ancestors ate manna in the desert, but they died. But the bread that comes down from heaven is of such a kind that whoever eats it will not die. I am the living bread that came down from heaven. If anyone eats this bread, he will live for ever. The bread that I will give him is my flesh, which I give so that the world may live.

And when these words started an angry argument among them, and they asked how this man could give them His flesh to eat
I am telling you the truth: if you do not eat the flesh of the Son of Man and drink his blood, you will not have life in yourselves. Whoever eats my flesh and drinks my blood has eternal life, and I will raise him to life on the last day. For my flesh is the real food; my blood is the real drink. Whoever eats my flesh and drinks my blood lives in me, and I live in him. The living Father sent me, and because of him I live also. In the same way whoever eats me will live because of me. This, then, is the bread

that came down from heaven; it is not like the bread that your ancestors ate, but then later died. The one who eats this bread will live for ever.

The Words of Eternal Life
Jn 6.61–64,65,67,70

When many of His followers decided that this teaching of His was too hard for them to listen to
Does this make you want to give up? Suppose, then, that you should see the Son of Man go back up to the place where he was before? What gives life is God's Spirit; man's power is of no use at all. The words I have spoken to you bring God's life-giving Spirit. Yet some of you do not believe.

And, knowing who were the ones who would not believe, and which one would betray Him
This is the very reason I told you that no one can come to me unless the Father makes it possible for him to do so.

To His twelve disciples when many of His followers had turned back
And you – would you also like to leave?

When Simon Peter said that they could only go to Him, Jesus, because His words gave eternal life, and they believed therefore that He was the Holy One, come from God
I chose the twelve of you, didn't I? Yet one of you is a devil!

Jesus and His Brothers
Jn 7.6–8

To His brothers when they tried to persuade Jesus to go openly to the festival in Judaea that all might see what He was doing
The right time for me has not yet come. Any time is right for you. The world cannot hate you, but it hates me, because I keep telling it that its ways are bad. You go on to the festival. I am not going to this festival, because the right time has not come for me.

Jesus at the Festival of Shelters
Jn 7.16–19,21–24

Later, when He went secretly to the festival, and taught in the Temple, surprising the Jewish authorities by His knowledge
What I teach is not my own teaching, but it comes from God, who sent me. Whoever is willing to do what God wants will know whether what I teach comes from God or whether I speak on my own authority. A person who speaks on his own authority is trying to gain glory for himself. But he who wants glory for the one who sent him is honest, and there is nothing false in him. Moses gave you the Law, didn't he? But not one of you obeys the Law. Why are you trying to kill me?

When the crowd exclaimed that He had a demon in Him, because He imagined someone was trying to kill Him
I performed one miracle, and you were all surprised. Moses ordered you to circumcise your sons (although it was not Moses but your ancestors who started it), and so you circumcise a boy on the Sabbath. If a boy is circumcised on the Sabbath so that Moses' Law is not broken, why are you angry with me because I made a man completely well on the Sabbath? Stop judging by external standards, and judge by true standards.

Is He the Messiah?
Jn 7.28–29

When some of the people of Jerusalem said that He could not be the Messiah because they all knew where He came from
Do you really know me and know where I am from? I have not come on my own authority. He who sent me, however, is truthful. You do not know him, but I know him, because I come from him and he sent me.

Guards Are Sent to Arrest Jesus
Jn 7.33–34

When some guards were sent by the Pharisees to arrest Jesus
I shall be with you a little while longer, and then I shall go away to him who sent me. You will look for me, but you will not find me, because you cannot go where I will be.

Streams of Life-Giving Water
Jn 7.37–38

On the last and most important day of the festival
Whoever is thirsty should come to me and drink. As the scripture says, 'Whoever believes in me, streams of life-giving water will pour out from his heart.'

The Woman Caught in Adultery
Jn 8.7,10,11

In the Temple next morning when the teachers of the Law and the Pharisees brought in a woman who had been caught in adultery, and asked Him whether they should not stone her, in accordance with the Law of Moses
Whichever one of you has committed no sin may throw the first stone at her.

When the crowd had gone away, leaving the woman alone there with Jesus
Where are they? Is there no one left to condemn you?

When she said that there was no one
Well, then, I do not condemn you either. Go, but do not sin again.

Jesus the Light of the World
Jn 8.12,14–18,19

To the Pharisees
I am the light of the world. Whoever follows me will have the light of life and will never walk in darkness.

When the Pharisees said that what Jesus said proved nothing because He was testifying on His own behalf
No, even though I do testify on my own behalf, what I say is true, because I know where I came from and where I am going. You do not know where I came from or where I am going. You make judgements in a purely human way; I pass judgement on no one. But if I were to do so, my judgement would be true, because I am not alone in this; the Father who sent me is with me. It is written in your Law that when two witnesses agree, what they say is true. I testify on my own behalf, and the Father who sent me also testifies on my behalf.

When they asked Him where His Father was
You know neither me nor my Father. If you knew me, you would know my Father also.

You Cannot Go Where I Am Going
Jn 8.21,23–24,25–26,28–29

To the Pharisees again
I will go away; you will look for me, but you will die in your sins. You cannot go where I am going.

When the Jewish authorities wondered whether He meant He would kill Himself
You belong to this world here below, but I come from above. You are from this world, but I am not from this world. That is why I told you that you will die in your sins. And you will die in your sins if you do not believe that 'I Am Who I Am'.

When they asked Him who He was
What I have told you from the beginning. I have much to say about you, much to condemn you for. The one who sent me, however, is truthful, and I tell the world only what I have heard from him.

When they did not understand that Jesus was talking about the Father
When you lift up the Son of Man, you will know that 'I Am Who I Am'; then you will know that I do nothing on my own authority, but I say only what the Father has instructed me to say. And he who sent me is with me; he has not left me alone, because I always do what pleases him.

Free Men and Slaves
Jn 8.31–32,34–38,39–41,42–47

To those who had heard Him and who believed in Him
If you obey my teaching, you are really my disciples; you will know the truth, and the truth will set you free.

When they said that they were Abraham's descendants and had never been slaves
I am telling you the truth: everyone who sins is a slave of sin. A slave does not belong to a family permanently, but a son belongs there for ever. If the Son sets you free, then you will be really free. I know you are Abraham's descendants. Yet you are trying to kill me, because you will not accept my teaching. I talk about what my Father has shown me, but you do what your father has told you.

When they told Him that their father was Abraham
If you really were Abraham's children, you would do the same things that he did. All I have ever done is to tell you the truth I heard from God, yet you are trying to kill me. Abraham did nothing like this! You are doing what your father did.

When the people then said that God Himself was their only Father, and they were His true sons
If God really were your Father, you would love me, because I came from God and now I am here. I did not come on my own authority, but he sent me. Why do you not understand what I say? It is because you cannot bear to listen to my message. You are the children of your father, the Devil, and you want to follow your father's desires. From the very beginning he was a murderer and has never been on the side of truth, because there is no truth in him. When he tells a lie, he is only doing what is natural to him, because he is a liar and the father of all lies. But I tell the truth, and that is why you do not believe me. Which one of you can prove that I am guilty of sins? If I tell the truth, then why do you not believe me? He who comes from God listens to God's words. You, however, are not from God, and that is why you will not listen.

Jesus and Abraham
Jn 8.49–51,54–56,58

When the people accused Him of being a Samaritan and possessed by a demon
I have no demon. I honour my Father, but you dishonour me. I am not seeking honour for myself. But there is one who is seeking it and who judges in my favour. I am telling you the truth: whoever obeys my teaching will never die.

When they objected to what He said
If I were to honour myself, that honour would be worth nothing. The one who honours me is my Father – the very one you say is your God. You have never known him, but I know him. If I were to say that I do not know him, I would be a liar like you. But I do know him, and I obey his word. Your father Abraham rejoiced that he was to see the time of my coming; he saw it and was glad.

When they asked Him how He could have seen Abraham when He was not even fifty years old
I am telling you the truth. Before Abraham was born, 'I Am'.

Jesus Heals a Man Born Blind
Jn 9.3–5,7

When His disciples asked whose sin had caused a man to be born blind
His blindness has nothing to do with his sins or his parents' sins. He is blind so that God's power might be seen at work in him. As long as it is day, we must keep on doing the work of him who sent me; night is coming when no one can work. While I am in the world, I am the light for the world.

After He had made some mud with earth and spittle and rubbed it on the man's eyes
Go and wash your face in the Pool of Siloam.

Spiritual Blindness
Jn 9.35,37,39,41

Later, when He discovered that the blind man had been expelled from the synagogue for believing that Jesus came from God
Do you believe in the Son of Man?

When the man asked who He was so that he could believe in Him
You have already seen him, and he is the one who is talking with you now.

When the man then said he believed and knelt before Jesus
I came to this world to judge, so that the blind should see and those who see should become blind.

When some Pharisees who heard these words asked whether He meant they were blind as well
If you were blind, then you would not be guilty; but since you claim that you can see, this means that you are still guilty.

The Parable of the Shepherd
Jn 10.1–5

As He told them a parable
I am telling you the truth: the man who does not enter the

sheepfold by the gate, but climbs in some other way, is a thief and a robber. The man who goes in through the gate is the shepherd of the sheep. The gatekeeper opens the gate for him; the sheep hear his voice as he calls his own sheep by name, and he leads them out. When he has brought them out, he goes ahead of them, and the sheep follow him, because they know his voice. They will not follow someone else; instead they will run away from such a person, because they do not know his voice.

Jesus the Good Shepherd
Jn 10.7–18

When they did not understand
I am telling you the truth: I am the gate for the sheep. All others who came before me are thieves and robbers, but the sheep did not listen to them. I am the gate. Whoever comes in by me will be saved; he will come in and go out and find pasture. The thief comes only in order to steal, kill, and destroy. I have come in order that you might have life – life in all its fullness.

I am the good shepherd, who is willing to die for the sheep. When the hired man, who is not a shepherd and does not own the sheep, sees a wolf coming, he leaves the sheep and runs away; so the wolf snatches the sheep and scatters them. The hired man runs away because he is only a hired man and does not care about the sheep. I am the good shepherd. As the Father knows me and I know the Father, in the same way I know my sheep and they know me. And I am willing to die for them. There are other sheep which belong to me that are not in this sheepfold, I must bring them, too; they will listen to my voice, and they will become one flock with one shepherd.

The Father loves me because I am willing to give up my life, in order that I may receive it back again. No one takes my life away from me. I give it up of my own free will. I have the right to give it up, and I have the right to take it back. This is what my Father has commanded me to do.

Jesus is Rejected
Jn 10.25–30,32,34–38

At the Festival of Dedication, in the Temple of Jerusalem, when the people asked Him to tell them plainly whether or not He was the Messiah
I have already told you, but you would not believe me. The things I do by my Father's authority speak on my behalf; but you will not believe, for you are not my sheep. My sheep listen

to my voice; I know them, and they follow me. I give them eternal life, and they shall never die. No one can snatch them away from me. What my Father has given me is greater than everything, and no one can snatch them away from the Father's care. The Father and I are one.

When the people picked up stones to throw at Him
I have done many good deeds in your presence which the Father gave me to do; for which one of these do you want to stone me?

In answer to their accusation of blasphemy
It is written in your own Law that God said, 'You are gods.' We know that what the scripture says is true for ever; and God called those people gods, the people to whom his message was given. As for me, the Father chose me and sent me into the world. How, then, can you say that I blaspheme because I said that I am the Son of God? Do not believe me, then, if I am not doing the things my Father wants me to do. But if I do them, even though you do not believe me, you should at least believe my deeds, in order that you may know once and for all that the Father is in me and that I am in the Father.

The Death of Lazarus
Jn 11.4,7,9–11,14–15

When He received a message from Mary and Martha that their brother, Lazarus, was ill
The final result of this illness will not be the death of Lazarus; this has happened in order to bring glory to God, and it will be the means by which the Son of God will receive glory.

To His disciples after He had remained where He was for two more days
Let us go back to Judaea.

When the disciples were worried that He might be stoned
A day has twelve hours, hasn't it? So whoever walks in broad daylight does not stumble for he sees the light of this world. But if he walks during the night he stumbles, because he has no light. Our friend Lazarus has fallen asleep, but I will go and wake him up.

When the disciples thought Jesus meant natural sleep, and that Lazarus was therefore recovering
Lazarus is dead, but for your sake I am glad that I was not with him, so that you will believe. Let us go to him.

Jesus the Resurrection and the Life Jn 11.23,25–26	*When Martha said she believed He could help her brother even though Lazarus had been buried for four days* Your brother will rise to life.
	When she said she knew Lazarus would rise on the last day I am the resurrection and the life. Whoever believes in me will live, even though he dies; and whoever lives and believes in me will never die. Do you believe this?
Jesus Weeps Jn 11.34	*To Mary and those weeping with her* Where have you buried him?
Lazarus Is Brought to Life Jn 11.39,40,41–42,43,44	*As He stood at the tomb, deeply moved* Take the stone away!
	When Martha said there would be a bad smell as Lazarus had been buried four days Didn't I tell you that you would see God's glory if you believed?
	When they had taken the stone away I thank you, Father, that you listen to me. I know that you always listen to me, but I say this for the sake of the people here, so that they will believe that you sent me.
	As He called to Lazarus Lazarus, come out!
	When Lazarus came out, still wrapped in his grave clothes Untie him, and let him go.
Jesus Is Anointed at Bethany Jn 12.7–8	*Six days before the Passover, when Mary anointed Jesus with an expensive perfume, and Judas Iscariot complained that the perfume should have been sold and the money given to the poor* Leave her alone! Let her keep what she has for the day of my burial. You will always have poor people with you, but you will not always have me.
Some Greeks Seek Jesus Jn 12.23–26	*To Philip and Andrew when some Greeks had asked to see Him* The hour has now come for the Son of Man to receive great glory. I am telling you the truth: a grain of wheat remains no more than a single grain unless it is dropped into the ground and dies. If it does die, then it produces many grains. Whoever loves his own life will lose it; whoever hates his own life in this

world will keep it for life eternal. Whoever wants to serve me must follow me, so that my servant will be with me where I am. And my Father will honour anyone who serves me.

Jesus Speaks about His Death
Jn 12.27–28,30–32,35–36

About His attitude to His death
Now my heart is troubled – and what shall I say? Shall I say, 'Father, do not let this hour come upon me'? But that is why I came – so that I might go through this hour of suffering. Father, bring glory to your name!

To the crowd, when a voice spoke from heaven in answer to His words
It was not for my sake that this voice spoke, but for yours. Now is the time for this world to be judged; now the ruler of this world will be overthrown. When I am lifted up from the earth, I will draw everyone to me.

When the crowd questioned this, not understanding who the Son of Man was, or why He should be lifted up, because they believed the Messiah would live for ever
The light will be among you a little longer. Continue on your way while you have the light, so that the darkness will not come upon you; for the one who walks in the dark does not know where he is going. Believe in the light, then, while you have it, so that you will be the people of the light.

Judgement by Jesus' Words
Jn 12.44–50

Whoever believes in me believes not only in me but also in him who sent me. Whoever sees me sees also him who sent me. I have come into the world as light, so that everyone who believes in me should not remain in the darkness. If anyone hears my message and does not obey it, I will not judge him. I came, not to judge the world, but to save it. Whoever rejects me and does not accept my message has one who will judge him. The words I have spoken will be his judge on the last day! This is true, because I have not spoken on my own authority, but the Father who sent me has commanded me what I must say and speak. And I know that his command brings eternal life. What I say, then, is what the Father has told me to say.

Jesus Washes His Disciples' Feet
Jn 13.7,8,10,12–20

When Simon Peter asked Him if He was going to wash his feet
You do not understand now what I am doing, but you will understand later.

When Peter declared that Jesus would never wash his feet
If I do not wash your feet, you will no longer be my disciple.

When Peter then asked Him to wash his hands and head also
Anyone who has had a bath is completely clean and does not have to wash himself, except his feet. All of you are clean – all except one.

When Jesus had washed their feet and returned to His place at the table
Do you understand what I have just done to you? You call me Teacher and Lord, and it is right that you do so, because that is what I am. I, your Lord and Teacher, have just washed your feet. You, then, should wash one another's feet. I have set an example for you, so that you will do just what I have done for you. I am telling you the truth: no slave is greater than his master, and no messenger is greater than the one who sent him. Now that you know this truth, how happy you will be if you put it into practice!

I am not talking about all of you; I know those I have chosen. But the scripture must come true that says, 'The man who shared my food turned against me.' I tell you this now before it happens, so that when it does happen, you will believe that 'I Am Who I Am.' I am telling you the truth: whoever receives anyone I send receives me also; and whoever receives me receives him who sent me.

Jesus Predicts His Betrayal
Jn 13.21,26,27

Openly to His disciples
I am telling you the truth: one of you is going to betray me.

When one of the disciples asked Him who it was
I will dip some bread in the sauce and give it to him; he is the man.

To Judas, to whom He had given the bread
Be quick about what you are doing!

The New Commandment
Jn 13.31–35

After Judas had accepted the bread and left at once
Now the Son of Man's glory is revealed; now God's glory is revealed through him. And if God's glory is revealed through him, then God will reveal the glory of the Son of Man in himself, and he will do so at once. My children, I shall not be with you very much longer. You will look for me; but I tell you now what

127

I told the Jewish authorities, 'You cannot go where I am going.' And now I give you a new commandment: love one another. As I have loved you, so you must love one another. If you have love for one another, then everyone will know that you are my disciples.

Jesus Predicts Peter's Denial
Jn 13.36,38

When Simon Peter asked Him where He was going
You cannot follow me now where I am going, but later you will follow me.

When Peter asked Him why he could not follow, saying he was ready to die for Him
Are you really ready to die for me? I am telling you the truth: before the cock crows you will say three times that you do not know me.

Jesus the Way to the Father
Jn 14.1–4,6–7,9–14

To His disciples
Do not be worried and upset. Believe in God and believe also in me. There are many rooms in my Father's house, and I am going to prepare a place for you. I would not tell you this if it were not so. And after I go and prepare a place for you, I will come back and take you to myself, so that you will be where I am. You know the way that leads to the place where I am going.

When Thomas told Jesus they could not know the way, because they did not know where He was going.
I am the way, the truth, and the life; no one goes to the Father except by me. Now that you have known me, you will know my Father also, and from now on you do know him and you have seen him.

When Philip asked Him to show them the Father
For a long time I have been with you all; yet you do not know me, Philip? Whoever has seen me has seen the Father. Why, then, do you say, 'Show us the Father'? Do you not believe, Philip, that I am in the Father and the Father is in me? The words that I have spoken to you do not come from me. The Father, who remains in me, does his own work. Believe me when I say that I am in the Father and the Father is in me. If not, believe because of the things I do. I am telling you the truth: whoever believes in me will do what I do – yes, he will do even greater things, because I am going to the Father. And I will do whatever you ask for in my name, so that the Father's glory will

be shown through the Son. If you ask me for anything in my name, I will do it.

The Promise of the Holy Spirit
Jn 14.15–21,23–31

If you love me, you will obey my commandments. I will ask the Father, and he will give you another Helper, who will stay with you for ever. He is the Spirit who reveals the truth about God. The world cannot receive him, because it cannot see him or know him. But you know him, because he remains with you and is in you.

When I go, you will not be left alone; I will come back to you. In a little while the world will see me no more, but you will see me; and because I live, you also will live. When that day comes, you will know that I am in my Father and that you are in me, just as I am in you.

Whoever accepts my commandments and obeys them is the one who loves me. My Father will love whoever loves me; I too will love him and reveal myself to him.

When Judas (not Judas Iscariot) asked how He would reveal Himself to them and not to the world
Whoever loves me will obey my teaching. My Father will love him, and my Father and I will come to him and live with him. Whoever does not love me does not obey my teaching. And the teaching you have heard is not mine but comes from the Father, who sent me.

I have told you this while I am still with you. The Helper, the Holy Spirit, whom the Father will send in my name, will teach you everything and make you remember all that I have told you.

Peace is what I leave with you; it is my own peace that I give you. I do not give it as the world does. Do not be worried and upset; do not be afraid. You heard me say to you, 'I am leaving, but I will come back to you.' If you loved me, you would be glad that I am going to the Father; for he is greater than I. I have told you this now before it all happens, so that when it does happen, you will believe. I cannot talk with you much longer, because the ruler of this world is coming. He has no power over me, but the world must know that I love the Father; that is why I do everything as he commands me.

Come, let us go from this place.

Jesus the Real Vine
Jn 15.1–17

I am the real vine, and my Father is the gardener. He breaks off every branch in me that does not bear fruit, and he prunes every branch that does bear fruit, so that it will be clean and bear more fruit. You have been made clean already by the teaching I have given you. Remain united to me, and I will remain united to you. A branch cannot bear fruit by itself; it can do so only if it remains in the vine. In the same way you cannot bear fruit unless you remain in me.

I am the vine, and you are the branches. Whoever remains in me, and I in him, will bear much fruit; for you can do nothing without me. Whoever does not remain in me is thrown out like a branch and dries up; such branches are gathered up and thrown into the fire, where they are burnt. If you remain in me and my words remain in you, then you will ask for anything you wish, and you shall have it. My Father's glory is shown by your bearing much fruit; and in this way you become my disciples. I love you just as the Father loves me; remain in my love. If you obey my commands, you will remain in my love, just as I have obeyed my Father's commands and remain in his love.

I have told you this so that my joy may be in you and that your joy may be complete. My commandment is this: love one another, just as I love you. The greatest love a person can have for his friends is to give his life for them. And you are my friends if you do what I command you. I do not call you servants any longer, because a servant does not know what his master is doing. Instead, I call you friends, because I have told you everything I have heard from my Father. You did not choose me; I chose you and appointed you to go and bear much fruit, the kind of fruit that endures. And so the Father will give you whatever you ask of him in my name. This, then, is what I command you: love one another.

The World's Hatred
Jn 15.18—16.4

If the world hates you, just remember that it has hated me first. If you belonged to the world, then the world would love you as its own. But I chose you from this world, and you do not belong to it; that is why the world hates you. Remember what I told you: 'No slave is greater than his master.' If they persecuted me, they will persecute you too; if they obeyed my teaching, they will obey yours too. But they will do all this to you because you are mine; for they do not know the one who sent me. They would not have been guilty of sin if I had not come and spoken to them; as it is, they no longer have any excuse for their sin. Whoever hates me hates my Father also. They would not have been guilty of sin if I had not done among them the things that no one else ever did; as it is, they have seen what I did, and they hate both me and my Father. This, however, was bound to happen so that what is written in their Law may come true: 'They hated me for no reason at all.'

The Helper will come – the Spirit, who reveals the truth about God and who comes from the Father. I will send him to you from the Father, and he will speak about me. And you, too, will speak about me, because you have been with me from the very beginning.

I have told you this, so that you will not give up your faith. You will be expelled from the synagogues, and the time will come when anyone who kills you will think that by doing this he is serving God. People will do these things to you because they have not known either the Father or me. But I have told you this, so that when the time comes for them to do these things, you will remember that I told you.

The Work of the Holy Spirit
Jn 16.4–15

I did not tell you these things at the beginning, for I was with you. But now I am going to him who sent me, yet none of you asks me where I am going. And now that I have told you, your hearts are full of sadness. But I am telling you the truth: it is better for you that I go away, because if I do not go, the Helper will not come to you. But if I do go away, then I will send him to you. And when he comes, he will prove to the people of the world that they are wrong about sin and about what is right and about God's judgement. They are wrong about sin, because they do not believe in me; they are wrong about what is right because I am going to the Father and you will not see me any more; and they are wrong about judgement, because the ruler of this world has already been judged.

I have much more to tell you, but now it would be too much for you to bear. When, however, the Spirit comes, who reveals the truth about God, he will lead you into all the truth. He will not speak on his own authority, but he will speak of what he hears, and will tell you of things to come. He will give me glory, because he will take what I say and tell it to you. All that my Father has is mine; that is why I said that the Spirit will take what I give him and tell it to you.

Sadness and Gladness
Jn 16.16,19–24

In a little while you will not see me any more, and then a little while later you will see me.

When the disciples questioned this among themselves
I said, 'In a little while you will not see me, and then a little while later you will see me.' Is this what you are asking about among yourselves? I am telling you the truth: you will cry and weep, but the world will be glad; you will be sad, but your sadness will turn into gladness. When a woman is about to give birth, she is sad because her hour of suffering has come; but when the baby is born, she forgets her suffering, because she is happy that a baby has been born into the world. That is how it is with you: now you are sad, but I will see you again, and your hearts will be filled with gladness, the kind of gladness that no one can take away from you.

When that day comes, you will not ask me for anything. I am telling you the truth: the Father will give you whatever you ask him for in my name. Until now you have not asked for anything in my name; ask and you will receive, so that your happiness may be complete.

Victory over the World
Jn 16.25–28,31–33

I have used figures of speech to tell you these things. But the time will come when I will not use figures of speech, but will speak to you plainly about the Father. When that day comes, you will ask him in my name; and I do not say that I will ask him on your behalf, for the Father himself loves you. He loves you because you love me and have believed that I came from God. I did come from the Father, and I came into the world; and now I am leaving the world and going to the Father.

When the disciples then said that now that He was speaking plainly they could believe that He came from God
Do you believe now? The time is coming, and is already here, when all of you will be scattered, each one to his own home, and I will be left all alone. But I am not really alone, because the Father is with me. I have told you this so that you will have

peace by being united to me. The world will make you suffer. But be brave! I have defeated the world!

Jesus Prays for His Disciples
Jn 17.1–26

To His Father in heaven
Father, the hour has come. Give glory to your Son, so that the Son may give glory to you. For you gave him authority over all mankind, so that he might give eternal life to all those you gave him. And eternal life means knowing you, the only true God, and knowing Jesus Christ, whom you sent. I have shown your glory on earth; I have finished the work you gave me to do. Father! Give me glory in your presence now, the same glory I had with you before the world was made.

I have made you known to those you gave me out of the world. They belonged to you, and you gave them to me. They have obeyed your word, and now they know that everything you gave me comes from you. I gave them the message that you gave me, and they received it; they know that it is true that I came from you, and they believe that you sent me.

I pray for them. I do not pray for the world but for those you gave me, for they belong to you. All I have is yours, and all you have is mine; and my glory is shown through them. And now I am coming to you; I am no longer in the world, but they are in the world. Holy Father! Keep them safe by the power of your name, the name you gave me, so that they may be one just as you and I are one. While I was with them, I kept them safe by the power of your name, the name you gave me. I protected them, and not one of them was lost, except the man who was bound to be lost – so that the scripture might come true. And now I am coming to you, and I say these things in the world so that they might have my joy in their hearts in all its fullness. I gave them your message, and the world hated them, because they do not belong to the world, just as I do not belong to the world. I do not ask you to take them out of the world, but I do ask you to keep them safe from the Evil One. Just as I do not belong to the world, they do not belong to the world. Dedicate them to yourself by means of the truth; your word is truth. I sent them into the world, just as you sent me into the world. And for their sake I dedicate myself to you, in order that they, too, may be truly dedicated to you.

I pray not only for them, but also for those who believe in me because of their message. I pray that they may all be one. Father! May they be in us, just as you are in me and I am in you. May they be one, so that the world will believe that you sent me. I gave them the same glory you gave me, so that they may be one, just as you and I are one: I in them and you in me, so that they may be completely one, in order that the world may know that you sent me and that you love them as you love me.

Father! You have given them to me, and I want them to be with me where I am, so that they may see my glory, the glory you gave me; for you loved me before the world was made. Righteous Father! The world does not know you, but I know you, and these know that you sent me. I made you known to them, and I will continue to do so, in order that the love you have for me may be in them, and so that I also may be in them.

The Arrest of Jesus
Jn 18.4,5,7,8,9,11

When Judas, accompanied by a band of armed Roman soldiers, came to Him in the garden
Who is it you are looking for?

When they said, 'Jesus of Nazareth'
I am he.

When they then moved back and fell to the ground
Who is it you are looking for?

When they again said it was Jesus of Nazareth
I have already told you that I am he. If, then, you are looking for me, let these others go.

Recalled by John to explain Jesus' attitude to the disciples
Father, I have not lost even one of those you gave me.

To Simon Peter who had cut off the right ear of the High Priest's slave
Put your sword back in its place! Do you think that I will not drink the cup of suffering which my Father has given me?

The High Priest Questions Jesus
Jn 18.20–21,23

When Jesus was brought before the High Priest and questioned about His disciples and His teaching
I have always spoken publicly to everyone; all my teaching was done in the synagogues and in the Temple, where all the people come together. I have never said anything in secret. Why, then,

do you question me? Question the people who heard me. Ask them what I told them – they know what I said.

When one of the guards then slapped Him for daring to talk to the High Priest in that way
If I have said anything wrong, tell everyone here what it was. But if I am right in what I have said, why do you hit me?

Jesus Is Brought Before Pilate
Jn 18.34,36,37

When Jesus was brought before Pilate who asked Him if He was the King of the Jews
Does this question come from you or have others told you about me?

When Pilate questioned Him further
My kingdom does not belong to this world; if my kingdom belonged to this world, my followers would fight to keep me from being handed over to the Jewish authorities. No, my kingdom does not belong here!

When Pilate asked Him if He was therefore a king
You say that I am a king. I was born and came into the world for this one purpose, to speak about the truth. Whoever belongs to the truth listens to me.

Jesus Is Sentenced To Death
Jn 18.11

When Pilate spoke about his own authority
You have authority over me only because it was given to you by God. So the man who handed me over to you is guilty of a worse sin.

Jesus Is Crucified
Jn 19.26,27

To His mother, when He saw her standing at the foot of the cross with the disciple He loved
He is your son.

To the disciple
She is your mother.

The Death of Jesus
Jn 19.28,30

From the cross, in order to make the scripture come true
I am thirsty.

When He had drunk the wine that was given to Him
It is finished!

Jesus Appears to Mary Magdalene
Jn 20.15,16,17

To Mary Magdalene, when He met her in the garden on the Sunday after His crucifixion
Woman, why are you crying? Who is it that you are looking for?

When she thought He was the gardener and asked Him to tell her where Jesus' body had been put
Mary!

When Mary recognized Him
Do not hold on to me because I have not yet gone back up to the Father. But go to my brothers and tell them that I am returning to him who is my Father and their Father, my God and their God.

Jesus Appears to His Disciples
Jn 20.19,21,22–23

Late that Sunday evening, when He came and stood among the disciples who were gathered together behind locked doors for fear of the Jewish authorities
Peace be with you.

When Jesus had showed them His hands and His side, and they were filled with joy at seeing Him
Peace be with you. As the Father sent me, so I send you.

As He breathed on the disciples
Receive the Holy Spirit. If you forgive people's sins, they are forgiven; if you do not forgive them, they are not forgiven.

Jesus and Thomas
Jn 20.26,27,29

A week later, when Jesus again came and stood among them, although the doors were locked
Peace be with you.

And then to Thomas, who had not been there the time before, and would not believe unless he could see the scars for himself
Put your finger here, and look at my hands; then stretch out your hand and put it in my side. Stop your doubting, and believe!

When Thomas exclaimed that He was his Lord and his God
Do you believe because you see me? How happy are those who believe without seeing me!

Jesus Appears to Seven Disciples
Jn 21.5,6,10,12

At Lake Tiberias, when seven of His disciples had been fishing all night and had caught nothing
Young men, haven't you caught anything?

When they said they had not caught a thing
Throw your net out on the right side of the boat, and you will catch some.

To the disciples who had now recognized Him and had come ashore with their catch of fish
Bring some of the fish you have just caught.

When Simon Peter had dragged the net ashore full of large fish
Come and eat.

Jesus and Peter
Jn 21.15,16,17,18,19

To Simon Peter, after they had eaten
Simon son of John, do you love me more than these others do?

When Peter said that the Lord knew that he loved Him
Take care of my lambs.

And a second time
Simon son of John, do you love me?

And when Peter answered again as he had before
Take care of my sheep.

And a third time
Simon son of John, do you love me?

When Peter was sad at being asked this a third time, and told Jesus that He knew everything, and that He knew that he loved Him
Take care of my sheep. I am telling you the truth: when you were young, you used to get ready and go anywhere you wanted to; but when you are old, you will stretch out your hands and someone else will bind you and take you where you don't want to go. Follow me!

Jesus and the Other Disciple
Jn 21.22

To Peter when he then asked what would happen to another disciple, the one whom Jesus loved
If I want him to live until I come, what is that to you? Follow me!

Appendix

Christ's Words

in Acts, Corinthians & Revelation

Christ's Words in Acts

Introduction
Acts 1.4–5

To His apostles, during the forty days after His death and resurrection and before His ascension
Do not leave Jerusalem, but wait for the gift I told you about, the gift my Father promised. John baptized with water, but in a few days you will be baptized with the Holy Spirit.

Jesus Is Taken up to Heaven
Acts 1.7–8

Just before His ascension, when the apostles asked Him whether He would at that time be giving the Kingdom back to Israel
The times and occasions are set by my Father's own authority, and it is not for you to know when they will be. But when the Holy Spirit comes upon you, you will be filled with power, and you will be witnesses for me in Jerusalem, in all Judaea and Samaria, and to the ends of the earth.

The Conversion of Saul
Acts 9.4,5–6,10,11–12,15–16

To Saul, when he was on his way to Damascus to arrest any Christians whom he might find there
Saul, Saul! Why do you persecute me?

When Saul asked who it was
I am Jesus, whom you persecute. But get up and go into the city, where you will be told what you must do.

Three days later in a vision to Ananias, a Christian in Damascus
Ananias!

When Ananias answered, 'Here I am, Lord'
Get ready and go to Straight Street, and at the house of Judas ask for a man from Tarsus named Saul. He is praying, and in a vision he has seen a man named Ananias come in and place his hands on him so that he might see again.

When Ananias said he knew Saul had been persecuting the Christians
Go, because I have chosen him to serve me, to make my name known to Gentiles and kings and to the people of Israel. And I myself will show him all that he must suffer for my sake.

Peter's Report to the Church at Jerusalem
Acts 11.16

Recalled by Peter, when the Holy Spirit came down on those in Cornelius' house
John baptized with water, but you will be baptized with the Holy Spirit.

In Corinth
Acts 18.9–10

In a vision to Paul when he was in Corinth
Do not be afraid, but keep on speaking and do not give up, for I am with you. No one will be able to harm you, for many in this city are my people.

Paul's Farewell Speech to the Elders of Ephesus
Acts 20.35

Recalled by Paul, when he was saying farewell to the elders of the church from Ephesus before he sailed for Jerusalem
There is more happiness in giving than in receiving.

Paul Tells of His Conversion
Acts 22.7,8,10

Recounted by Paul when he was defending his faith before the mob in Jerusalem
Saul, Saul! Why do you persecute me?

I am Jesus of Nazareth, whom you persecute.

Get up and go into Damascus, and there you will be told everything that God has determined for you to do.

Paul's Call to Preach to the Gentiles
Acts 22.18,21

Related by Paul, when talking about his vision in Jerusalem
Hurry and leave Jerusalem quickly, because the people here will not accept your witness about me.

Go, for I will send you far away to the Gentiles.

Paul before the Council
Acts 23.11

Later to Paul, after he had been brought before the Council
Don't be afraid! You have given your witness for me here in Jerusalem, and you must also do the same in Rome.

Paul Tells of His Conversion
Acts 26.14,15–18

Related by Paul when making his defence in front of King Agrippa in Caesarea, before being taken to Rome
Saul, Saul! Why are you persecuting me? You are hurting yourself by hitting back, like an ox kicking against its owner's stick.

I am Jesus, whom you persecute. But get up and stand on your feet. I have appeared to you to appoint you as my servant. You are to tell others what you have seen of me today and what I will show you in the future. I will rescue you from the people of Israel and from the Gentiles to whom I will send you. You are to open their eyes and turn them from the darkness to the light and from the power of Satan to God, so that through their faith in me they will have their sins forgiven and receive their place among God's chosen people.

Christ's Words in Corinthians

The Lord's Supper
1 Cor 11.24,25

Recalled by Paul, when he was writing to the Corinthian Christians about the Lord's Supper
This is my body, which is for you. Do this in memory of me.

This cup is God's new covenant, sealed with my blood. Whenever you drink it, do so in memory of me.

Paul's Visions and Revelations
2 Cor 12.9

To Paul when he prayed for a painful physical ailment to be taken away
My grace is all you need, for my power is strongest when you are weak.

Christ's Words in Revelation

A Vision of Christ
Rev 1.11,17–20

When He revealed Himself to John on the island of Patmos
Write down what you see, and send the book to the churches in these seven cities: Ephesus, Smyrna, Pergamum, Thyatira, Sardis, Philadelphia, and Laodicea.

When John saw Him and fell at His feet
Don't be afraid! I am the first and the last. I am the living one! I was dead, but now I am alive for ever and ever. I have authority over death and the world of the dead. Write, then, the things you see, both the things that are now and the things that will happen afterwards. This is the secret meaning of the seven stars that you see in my right hand, and of the seven gold lampstands: the seven stars are the angels of the seven churches, and the seven lamp-stands are the seven churches.

The Message to Ephesus
Rev 2.1–7

To the angel of the church in Ephesus write:
This is the message from the one who holds the seven stars in his right hand and who walks among the seven gold lamp-stands. I know what you have done; I know how hard you have worked and how patient you have been. I know that you cannot tolerate evil men and that you have tested those who say they are apostles but are not, and have found out that they are liars. You are patient, you have suffered for my sake, and you have not given up. But this is what I have against you: you do not love me now as you did at first. Think how far you have fallen! Turn from your sins and do what you did at first. If you don't turn from your sins, I will come to you and take your lamp-stand from its place. But this is what you have in your favour: you hate what the Nicolaitans do, as much as I do.

If you have ears, then, listen to what the Spirit says to the churches!

To those who win the victory I will give the right to eat the fruit of the tree of life that grows in the Garden of God.

The Message to Smyrna
Rev 2.8–11

To the angel of the church in Smyrna write:
This is the message from the one who is the first and the last, who died and lived again. I know your troubles; I know that you

are poor – but really you are rich! I know the evil things said against you by those who claim to be Jews but are not; they are a group that belongs to Satan! Don't be afraid of anything you are about to suffer. Listen! The Devil will put you to the test by having some of you thrown into prison, and your troubles will last ten days. Be faithful to me, even if it means death, and I will give you life as your prize of victory.

If you have ears, then, listen to what the Spirit says to the churches!

Those who win the victory will not be hurt by the second death.

The Message to Pergamum
Rev 2.12–17

To the angel of the church in Pergamum write:
This is the message from the one who has the sharp two-edged sword. I know where you live, there where Satan has his throne. You are true to me, and you did not abandon your faith in me even during the time when Antipas, my faithful witness, was killed there where Satan lives. But there are a few things I have against you: there are some among you who follow the teaching of Balaam, who taught Balak how to lead the people of Israel into sin by persuading them to eat food that had been offered to idols and to practise sexual immorality. In the same way you have people among you who follow the teaching of the Nicolaitans. Now turn from your sins! If you don't, I will come to you soon and fight against those people with the sword that comes out of my mouth.

If you have ears, then, listen to what the Spirit says to the churches!

To those who win the victory I will give some of the hidden manna. I will also give each of them a white stone on which is written a new name that no one knows except the one who receives it.

The Message to Thyatira
Rev 2.18–29

To the angel of the church in Thyatira write:
This is the message from the Son of God, whose eyes blaze like fire, whose feet shine like polished brass. I know what you do. I know your love, your faithfulness, your service, and your patience. I know that you are doing more now than you did at first. But this is what I have against you: you tolerate that woman Jezebel, who calls herself a messenger of God. By her

teaching she misleads my servants into practising sexual immorality and eating food that has been offered to idols. I have given her time to repent of her sins but she does not want to turn from her immorality. And so I will throw her on to a bed where she and those who committed adultery with her will suffer terribly. I will do this now unless they repent of the wicked things they did with her. I will also kill her followers, and then all the churches will know that I am the one who knows everyone's thoughts and wishes. I will repay each one of you according to what he has done.

But the rest of you in Thyatira have not followed this evil teaching; you have not learnt what the others call 'the deep secrets of Satan.' I say to you that I will not put any other burden on you. But until I come, you must hold firmly to what you have. To those who win the victory, who continue to the end to do what I want, I will give the same authority that I received from my Father: I will give them authority over the nations, to rule them with an iron rod and to break them to pieces like clay pots. I will also give them the morning star.

If you have ears, then, listen to what the Spirit says to the churches!

The Message to Sardis
Rev 3.1–6

To the angel of the church in Sardis write:
This is the message from the one who has the seven spirits of God and the seven stars. I know what you are doing; I know that you have the reputation of being alive, even though you are dead! So wake up, and strengthen what you still have before it dies completely. For I find that what you have done is not yet perfect in the sight of my God. Remember, then, what you were taught and what you heard; obey it and turn from your sins. If you do not wake up, I will come upon you like a thief, and you will not even know the time when I will come. But a few of you there in Sardis have kept your clothes clean. You will walk with me, clothed in white, because you are worthy to do so. Those who win the victory will be clothed like this in white, and I will not remove their names from the book of the living. In the presence of my Father and of his angels I will declare openly that they belong to me.

If you have ears, then, listen to what the Spirit says to the churches!

The Message to Philadelphia
Rev 3.7–13

To the angel of the church in Philadelphia write:

This is the message from the one who is holy and true. He has the key that belonged to David, and when he opens a door, no one can close it, and when he closes it, no one can open it. I know what you do; I know that you have a little power; you have followed my teaching and have been faithful to me. I have opened a door in front of you, which no one can close. Listen! As for that group that belongs to Satan, those liars who claim that they are Jews but are not, I will make them come and bow down at your feet. They will all know that I love you. Because you have kept my command to endure, I will also keep you safe from the time of trouble which is coming upon the world to test all the people on earth. I am coming soon. Keep safe what you have, so that no one will rob you of your victory prize. I will make him who is victorious a pillar in the temple of my God, and he will never leave it. I will write on him the name of my God and the name of the city of my God, the new Jerusalem, which will come down out of heaven from my God. I will also write on him my new name.

If you have ears, then, listen to what the Spirit says to the churches!

The Message to Laodicea
Rev 3.14–22

To the angel of the church in Laodicea write:

This is the message from the Amen, the faithful and true witness, who is the origin of all that God has created. I know what you have done; I know that you are neither cold nor hot. How I wish you were either one or the other! But because you are lukewarm, neither hot nor cold, I am going to spit you out of my mouth! You say, 'I am rich and well off; I have all I need.' But you do not know how miserable and pitiful you are! You are poor, naked, and blind. I advise you, then, to buy gold from me, pure gold, in order to be rich. Buy also white clothing to dress yourself and cover up your shameful nakedness. Buy also some ointment to put on your eyes, so that you may see. I rebuke and punish all whom I love. Be in earnest, then, and turn from your sins. Listen! I stand at the door and knock; if anyone hears my voice and opens the door, I will come into his house and eat with him, and he will eat with me. To those who win the victory I will give the right to sit beside me on my throne, just as I have been victorious and now sit by my Father on his throne.

If you have ears, then, listen to what the Spirit says to the churches!

The Coming of Jesus
Rev 22.7,12–13,16

At the end of the revelation, and after John had been shown many visions
Listen! I am coming soon! Happy are those who obey the prophetic words in this book!

Listen! I am coming soon! I will bring my rewards with me, to give to each one according to what he has done. I am the first and the last, the beginning and the end.

I, Jesus, have sent my angel to announce these things to you in the churches. I am descended from the family of David; I am the bright morning star.

Conclusion
Rev 22.20

After John had warned against anyone adding or taking away anything from the prophetic words of the book
Yes indeed! I am coming soon!